INTERNATIONAL DEVELOPMENT IN FOCUS

Skills and the Labor Market in a New Era

Managing the Impacts of Population Aging and Technological Change in Uruguay

IGNACIO APELLA, RAFAEL ROFMAN, AND HELENA ROVNER

Contents

Acknowledgments

This book has been prepared by a World Bank team, with members from the Social Protection and Jobs, Education, and Poverty and Equity Global Practices. The book was directed by Ignacio Apella (social protection specialist), Rafael Rofman (human development program leader), and Helena Rovner (senior education specialist); the team included Lourdes Rodriguez Chamussy (poverty economist), Valeria Bolla (communications officer), Emiliano Pereiro (Plan Ceibal), and consultants Diego Aboal, Fedora Carbajal, Emiliano Tealde, Caterina Colombo, Veronica Dalto, Andrés López, Roxana Maurizio, Paz Queraltó, and Gonzalo Zunino. The preparation, drafting, translating, and editing had the invaluable support of Florencia Chaves, Luciana García, and Marcela Stewart.

Background documents, as well as earlier versions of the report, were discussed in informal conversations and workshops with colleagues and counterparts in Uruguay. The final version received excellent comments from Rita Almeida, Omar Arias, and Truman Packard. Preparing this book was possible thanks to the leadership and support of Jesko Hentschel, Pablo Gottret, and Matilde Bordon.

The team is deeply grateful to all the aforementioned. Any mistakes or omissions remain the sole responsibility of the book's authors.

About the Authors

Ignacio Apella is an economist in the Social Protection and Jobs Global Practice at the World Bank. He has worked mainly on social protection, pension policy, labor economics, and health economics in Argentina, Bolivia, Chile, Ecuador, El Salvador, Mexico, Peru, Paraguay, and Uruguay. He is the author of many papers, journal articles, and books on social security, pension systems, and the labor market. He is also a professor of microeconomics at the University of Buenos Aires. He has an economics degree from the University of Buenos Aires and an MA in economics from the University of Buenos Aires.

Rafael Rofman is a program leader for Human Development in Argentina, Paraguay, and Uruguay at the World Bank. He has been a social protection lead specialist at the World Bank and was an independent researcher on aging and social security policies. He has published numerous papers and books and has taught at the University of California at Berkeley, New York University, University of Buenos Aires, University of Lujan, University Di Tella, and others. He has a degree in economics from the University of Buenos Aires, an MA in demography from National University of Lujan, and a PhD in demography from University of California at Berkeley.

Helena Rovner is a senior education specialist at the World Bank. Since she joined the Bank, she has led education projects in Argentina, Paraguay, and Uruguay. Before joining the World Bank, she worked in the Plan Ceibal in Uruguay, the national EdTech organization, leading the Monitoring and Evaluation Department, focusing on evaluation of design and implementation of projects related to adaptive learning software, remote teaching strategies, and measurement of digital skills and learning. She was a consultant at UNDP in the Regional Bureau for Latin America and the Caribbean, working for several countries in the Regional Human Development Reports Team. She has a PhD in government from the University of Essex.

Abbreviations

ATM	automated teller machine
BROU	Banco de la República Oriental del Uruguay
CHS	Continuous Household Survey
GDP	gross domestic product
ICT	information and communication technology
O*NET	Occupational Information Network
PISA	Program for International Student Assessment

Introduction

Uruguay, like many other countries in the region, faces serious medium- and long-term challenges associated with two global megatrends: population aging and technological change. These phenomena are closely related: an aging population and the resulting workforce reduction can be counterbalanced with the higher productivity that results from new, automation-based production technologies. These two trends have been developing for some time, but policy responses have been late or inadequate in many cases. Trying to delay them (by promoting higher fertility or enforcing restrictions on the adoption of new technology) would not only be ineffective but ill-advised, because these trends generate important opportunities to increase production and welfare. The objective of this book is to identify these opportunities, as well as the challenges that population aging and technological change pose for the Uruguayan economy, and to determine how they can be addressed through better-designed public policies.

As a consequence of demographic transition, Uruguay's population is gradually aging. The number of children is declining, the number of the elderly is growing, and its population is slowly converging to a stable, older structure in the long term. Unlike other countries in Latin America and the Caribbean, Uruguay is well advanced in its transition, which started in the middle of the 20th century. One of the challenges the country faces in this demographic process is to maintain the economic growth that will improve the population's welfare. Economic growth depends on the endowment of productive factors, work and capital (both physical and human), as well as total factor productivity. A decline in the active-age population may reduce the capacity for growth unless other factors increase to offset it.

Although medium-term dependency rates are expected to grow, the demographic dividend affords the country a great opportunity. This dividend emerges during a period when the share of the working-age population with savings capacity in the total population is at its highest levels, because the proportion of children is decreasing faster than the proportion of the elderly is increasing. Taking advantage of this opportunity means accumulating enough human and physical capital to increase productivity in a sustainable way in the medium and long term.

The demographic transition is taking place hand in hand with another global trend: technological change and task automation. This is particularly important because of the possibilities that technical change offers to achieve global productivity increases in the economy. Innovations such as the development of digital technologies and robotics may create gains in economic efficiency in the global economy. Nonetheless, this process also poses challenges for labor markets. In particular, without effective public policies designed to exploit the opportunities and mitigate the risks it creates, technological improvement may lead to a polarization of the labor market and deepen inequality.

As productive sectors adopt technological innovations, labor demand should decline. Automation-based productive processes take over routine tasks traditionally performed by workers, resulting in a "substitution effect" that lowers the demand for labor. However, improvements in efficiency could lead to cost and price reductions, increased demand, and, consequently, increased production and employment, generating a "scale effect." The net outcome will depend on which of these two effects is greater. The international empirical literature and two case studies for Uruguay (discussed in chapter 3 in the section titled "Definition of Technological Change and Measurement Methods"), suggest that the implementation of technological innovations has not had a significant impact on employment at the aggregate level, although it has led to changes in its structure. The Uruguayan labor market appears to be undergoing an incipient process of labor polarization that might produce negative distributive effects in the medium term.

To take advantage of opportunities created by innovative technologies, workers need skills that allow them to perform efficiently in a new productive environment. The literature shows that the critical skills most highly in demand in coming years will be not technical, but high-order cognitive and socioemotional. Hence, the education system in Uruguay should focus on providing these skills to the new generations that will join the labor force. Institutions that offer lifelong learning services should also develop effective reskilling programs.

Finally, labor regulations and social protection policies have an important role in labor market arrangements in this new context. On the one hand, regulations may hamper valuable innovations by interfering with the introduction of productive processes that did not exist when those regulations were drafted. On the other hand, governments must provide adequate protection to their citizens that recognizes ongoing changes in the market through effective social protection programs and by reducing asymmetries in labor contracts.

This book contains five chapters. Chapter 1 discusses the demographic trends and explains how they motivate the analysis. Chapter 2 presents a conceptual framework for the different dimensions discussed in the book, and chapter 3 focuses on Uruguay, describing the recent evolution and current context. Chapter 4 offers a review of policies that authorities might implement for the issues discussed, and chapter 5 summarizes the conclusions.

1 Demographic Trends as a Motivation

DEMOGRAPHIC TRENDS

As in most countries around the world, the Uruguayan population is undergoing a demographic transition, resulting in a gradual aging of its population, with a decrease in the number of children, an increase in the number of the elderly, and a general trend toward the stabilization of its population structure in the long term. This transition is the result of two positive social phenomena: declining mortality and fertility, caused by better health conditions and the higher capacity of women and men to decide on the final size of their families.

By 1908, the total global fertility rate was at a pretransitional level, with values of approximately six children per woman. As shown in figure 1.1, during the first half of the 20th century this value declined to approximately three children per woman and, since 1975, a new decline started, leading to current levels approximating population replacement. Mortality decline began earlier, in the 19th century, and life expectancy at birth already showed significant increases before 1900. This trend continued throughout the 20th century (with some slowing down in the 1970s), and today life expectancy at birth is above 75 years. Projections for the next decades assume that fertility will continue to decline until the middle of the century, and will then recover and stabilize slightly below the replacement level, while mortality will continue its decline and life expectancy at birth will reach 86 years by 2100.

The impact of this demographic change can be seen in the evolution of dependency rates. These indicators show the child dependency rate (the number of children under the age of 15 per 100 people age 15 to 64), the old-age dependency rate (the number of persons age 65 and older per 100 people age 15 to 64), and the total dependency rate, which includes both. Figure 1.2 shows the declining trend of child dependency and the increasing trend of old-age dependency. The second effect will prevail, and the total rate increases in the long term but with a temporary period of decline, known as the "demographic bonus," in the early decades of the 21st century. More specifically, this period has the lowest proportion of population dependent on others' income and, therefore, an opportunity to increase national savings.

Total global fertility rate and life expectancy at birth, 1850–2100

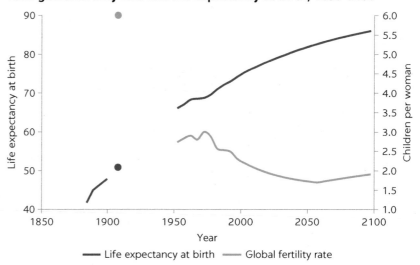

Source: Rofman, Amarante, and Apella 2016.
Note: Data from 1900 to 1950 are unavailable.

FIGURE 1.2

Demographic dependency ratio, 1950–2100

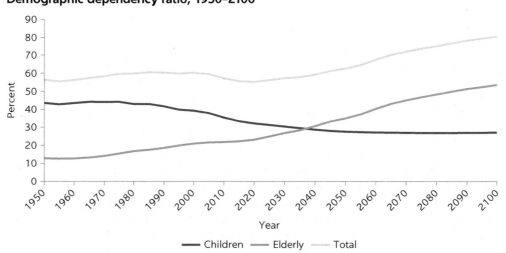

Source: World Bank estimates based on United Nations 2017.

DEMOGRAPHY AND ECONOMIC GROWTH

The effects of the demographic transition on economic growth are associated with what Lee and Mason (2006) call the first and second demographic dividend. The first dividend occurs when the share of the working-age population in relation to other age groups increases (in figure 1.2, between 2000 and 2020). This first dividend will start declining as the dependency rate increases (starting in 2020) and will disappear in 20 years.

The second demographic dividend takes place because of an increase in the share of the population that can be considered "prime savers" (that is, their levels of disposable income exceed their consumption expenditures) during the first dividend period. This leads to an increase in the economy's savings rate, which can be used to increase investments and productivity once the aging stage has been reached. The second demographic dividend is associated with the potential for greater accumulation of physical and human capital. The first dividend is transitory, while the second dividend yields long-term benefits through increased growth in production and sustainable development (see box 1.1).

Because the demographic trend is one of the forces driving economic growth, progress is likely to slow down as the first demographic dividend ends. However, labor market dynamics may offset this process, at least partially, if participation rates among those of working age increase. Figure 1.3 shows, for 1995 and 2016, the economically active population.

In the last twenty years participation rates declined for young adults (age 14 to 30), remained stable for those age 30 to 50, and increased among people age 50 or older. The lower participation of the young population shows that students stay longer in the education system, accumulating human capital (Apella and Troiano 2015). The increase in participation among older adults can be explained by several factors, including the incentives to continue working generated by the social security system, a wealth effect, the incidence of

---

BOX 1.1

Impact of the demographic dividend on Uruguay's economic growth

To better understand the impact of demographic dynamics on Uruguay's economic growth, this box shows a factorial decomposition exercise on gross domestic product (GDP) per capita. This exercise estimates the contribution of primary production factors and the contribution of total factor productivity. Specifically, the following aggregate production function is assumed:

$$Y = A.K^{\alpha}.(h.L)^{1-\alpha} \qquad (1)$$

Where:

Y is GDP

A is total factor productivity (TFP)

K is capital stock

L is labor force

h is human capital per worker

α is the share of returns to capital in GDP

Dividing (1) by size of the population N, GDP per capita is:

$$\frac{Y}{N} = A.\left(\frac{K}{L}\right)^{\alpha}.h^{1-\alpha}.\frac{L}{N_w}.\frac{N_w}{N} \qquad (2)$$

$$y = A.k^{\alpha}.h^{1-\alpha}.m.l$$

Where:

k is capital stock per worker

$m = \dfrac{L}{N_w}$ is the employment rate, where N_w is the population age between 15 and 64

$l = \dfrac{N_w}{N}$ represents the support ratio, that is, the inverse of the dependency ratio.

Economic growth can be measured as the rate of per capita increase in GDP. This rate can be disaggregated into its components. Using logarithm and differentiating equation (2) in relation to time, the variation can be factorized as follows, where $g(.)$ represents the growth rate:

$$g(y) = g(A) + \alpha.g(k) + (1-\alpha) * g(h) + g(m) + g(l) \qquad (3)$$

According to this factorization, it is possible to identify the contribution of the first dividend to growth: $g(m_r)$. Additionally, the forces that lead to a potential second dividend are associated with savings incentives during the demographic window of opportunity and with the changing weight of the saving cohorts. Because, unlike the first dividend, the second dividend operates through savings and accumulation of capital,

continued

Box 1.1, *continued*

its impact would be reflected in a greater dynamism of labor productivity and total factor productivity. This means that the second dividend occurs only if saving behaves to allow capital endowment to grow faster than the number of effective workers during the window of opportunity. Figure B1.1.1 shows the results of the factorization exercise on GDP per capita growth for Uruguay during the 1990–2014 period.

Results confirm the importance of the first dividend in the explanation of economic growth.

Before the beginning of the bonus in the late 20th century, the contribution of demography to economic growth was negative. However, since 2000, the demographic factor has contributed an average of 0.40 percentage point to the per capita growth of GDP. Of course, there are other factors that affect growth—such as capital stock per worker, human capital, employment level, and total factor productivity—which play different roles depending on the period of analysis considered.

FIGURE B1.1.1

Factorial decomposition of the GDP per capita growth rate, 1990–2014

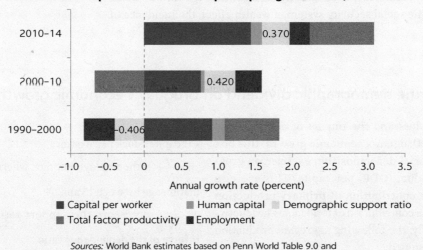

Sources: World Bank estimates based on Penn World Table 9.0 and United Nations 2017.

disability or inability to work, or the desire to continue working (Bertranou and Mastrángelo 2003).

Demographic changes should result in a decline in labor force participation rates in the medium term, if age-specific rates remain constant, as shown in figure 1.4. If no changes in behavior occur, demography would lead to a reduction in the support ratio of the economy. However, the trends observed in the last two decades show changes that might be intensified in the future, particularly within two population groups with low activity rates—women and older adults.

Although women's participation in the labor market has significantly increased over the last twenty years, it is still well below that of men. This suggests that Uruguay has an unexploited economic asset with great potential, even though human capital gaps by gender have closed and even reversed. The main barriers to female participation seem to be the unequal division of household responsibilities (including lack of effective child and older-adult care) and

FIGURE 1.3

Labor force participation rates in Uruguay, 1995 and 2016

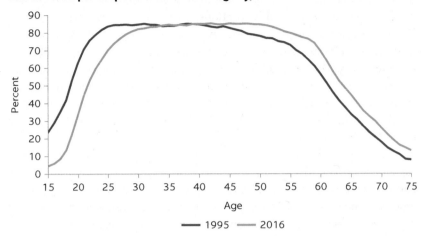

Source: World Bank estimates based on the Continuous Household Survey (CHS).

FIGURE 1.4

Projection of labor force participation rates, 2015–2100

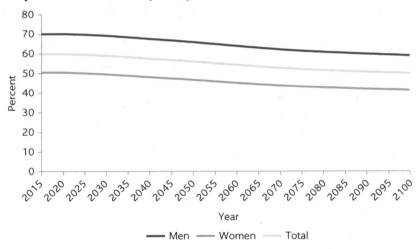

Sources: World Bank, based on the CHS and United Nations 2017.
Note: Assuming no changes in age-specific rates.

explicit or implicit employment-related discrimination. In several countries, achievements in these areas have been made through the implementation of quality and affordable child and elder-care services, paternity or shared parental leave, and active policies designed to reduce discrimination in the labor market.[1]

Regarding older adults, a delay of the retirement age is taking place naturally as individuals reach their 60s with a greater stock of human capital and jobs that demand fewer physically intense tasks. Colombo (2012) estimated that between 2004 and 2011 the retirement age increased by one year among men and by 0.5 year among women in Uruguay, reaching 63.6 and 61.9 years, respectively. This trend could continue in the future, especially if a favorable regulatory framework with financial incentives and flexibility for gradual retirement is adopted.

As in any decision-making process, two sets of factors condition the choice of individuals to remain in the labor market: preferences, reflecting individuals' desire to stay or retire; and restrictions, reflecting the availability of other income-generation options to finance everyday consumption. Preferences tend to affect decisions of higher-productivity workers, but restrictions usually have a greater impact on less-qualified, lower-productivity employees. Additionally, retirement decisions are usually the result of a process that requires some time. Inflexible labor arrangements probably lead workers to retire, even though they would be willing to continue working (and, consequently, contributing to the economy) if they could reduce their number of working hours.

The second source of per capita GDP growth is the increase in the ratio of capital per worker, which is associated with the second demographic dividend. Following Mason and Lee (2011), the second dividend has positive effects on growth, through increased savings and the resulting accumulation of physical capital and foreign assets. As the capital per worker ratio increases, productivity grows, and as the stock of foreign assets grows, domestic income improves. The second dividend will occur only if the capital endowment (which, in turn, depends on savings) grows faster than the number of workers during the first dividend period.

Uruguay has benefited from the first dividend, but it does not seem to be generating the necessary conditions for the second. Domestic savings rates have been low in recent decades, especially when compared to other countries that have experienced more effective growth paths (figure 1.5), and although the rate increased as the first dividend affected the economy, the increased level seems to be far from that needed for fast capital accumulation. If savings rates do not increase significantly in the next few years, the sustainability of economic growth will be at risk in the medium and long term, as dependency ratios increase.

FIGURE 1.5

Domestic saving rates as a percentage of GDP in selected countries, 1985–2017

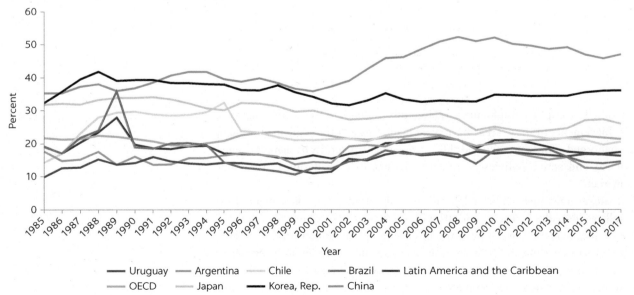

Source: World Bank 2019.
Note: OECD = Organisation for Economic Co-operation and Development.

A third channel of growth is linked to total factor productivity. Productivity played a leading role in economic growth in Uruguay from 2011 to 2015. However, a significant part of this contribution could be associated with the exploitation of natural resources (such as forest resources), which had historically played a very limited role. The process of technological change in Uruguay and the rest of the world is a potential source of productivity growth. However, this process poses challenges for the labor market. The following chapters discuss the interactions between technological change and the labor market and consider the challenges and opportunities that must be addressed by public policy.

NOTE

1. Uruguay launched a National Care System (Sistema Nacional de Cuidados) in 2015, to organize a system that would provide adequate care—through public, private, and family arrangements—to children and the elderly. The system is still in the early stages of development.

REFERENCES

Apella, I., and S. Troiano. 2015. "The Argentine Labor Market in a Context of Demographic Transition." In *As Time Goes By in Argentina: Economic Opportunities and Challenges of the Demographic Transition*, Directions in Development, edited by M. Gragnolati, R. Rofman, I. Apella, I., and S. Troiano, 319–50. Buenos Aires: World Bank. https://openknowledge.worldbank.org/handle/10986/21769.

Bertranou, F., and J. Mastrángelo. 2003. "Envejecimiento, trabajo, retiro y seguridad social en Chile." *IV International Research Conference on Social Security*. Antwerp.

Colombo, C. 2012. "Análisis de las principales características de las altas de jubilación de los años 2002 al 2011." *Comentarios de Seguridad Social 35*. Montevideo: Banco de Previsión Social. https://www.bps.gub.uy/bps/file/1414/1/altas-de-jubilacion-de-los-anos-2002-al-2011 .-colombo.-febrero-2012.pdf.

Lee, R., and A. Mason. 2006. "What is the Demographic Dividend?" *Finance and Development* 43 (3). http://www.imf.org/external/pubs/ft/fandd/2006/09/basics.htm.

Mason, A., and R. Lee. 2011. "Generational Economics in a Changing World." *Population and Development Review* 37 (s1): 115–42. https://www.ncbi.nlm.nih.gov/pmc/articles/PMC 3143474/.

Mason, A., R. Lee, and S-H. Lee. 2006. "Charting the Economic Life Cycle." NBER Working Paper 12379, National Bureau of Economic Research, Cambridge, MA. https://www.nber .org/papers/w12379.pdf.

Rofman, R., V. Amarante, and I. Apella. 2016. *Demographic Change in Uruguay: Economic Opportunities and Challenges*. Directions in Development. Washington, DC: World Bank. https://openknowledge.worldbank.org/handle/10986/24358.

United Nations. 2017. *World Population Prospects: The 2017 Revision, Volume I—Comprehensive Tables* (ST/ESA/SER.A/399). New York: United Nations. https://population.un.org/wpp /Publications/Files/WPP2017_Volume-I_Comprehensive-Tables.pdf.

World Bank. 2019. *World Development Indicators*. Washington, DC: World Bank. https:// databank.worldbank.org/reports.aspx?source=world-development-indicators.

2 Conceptual Framework

This chapter presents the conceptual framework discussed in the literature on the links between technological change and labor markets, and the impact and interactions that those links have on human capital accumulation and labor regulations. First, a clear definition of technological change is proposed; this concept has been used in the literature to refer to different processes. The second section of the chapter focuses on reviewing the conceptual frameworks and empirical findings (mostly in developed countries) supporting the discussion. The third and fourth sections address the impact of technological change on labor polarization and on a phenomenon that could be of relevance when discussing policies: aging of tasks. Then—recognizing the logical links behind technological change, labor tasks, and workers' skills—a discussion of the literature about skills and the existing mechanisms for their development is presented. Finally, the last section of the chapter focuses on the connection between technology-induced labor market changes and labor and social security regulatory and institutional frameworks.

DEFINITION OF TECHNOLOGICAL CHANGE AND MEASUREMENT METHODS

The concept of technological change is generally associated with task automation. However, technological change is a much broader notion that encompasses different channels and mechanisms. It comprises both "hard" innovations, such as the introduction of new or significantly improved products (including goods and services) and processes, and "soft" innovations, which include management, organization, and marketing.[1] Current discussions of technological change and the labor market focus on the impact of new automated processes. Therefore, this discussion focuses on "hard" innovations, although automation per se may lead to the need for organizational changes that have their own repercussions in employment (Evangelista and Vezzani 2012).

Product innovation includes completely new goods or services, changes in design, improvements in quality or performance, introduction of new functionalities, and replacement of components of existing products.

Improvements in services can include changes in the way services are provided (increasing efficiency or speed); upgrades (such as to software); new combinations (such as tour packages); or the introduction of new features (such as new functionalities in an automated teller machine—ATM) or equipment (such as individual screens in air transportation service) into existing services.

Process innovation is associated with the introduction of new (or significantly improved) equipment, techniques, procedures, and software used in the productive process, as well as changes in input provisioning, internal logistics, and final product distribution mechanisms. Automation processes fall within this category of technological change, as physical or digital robots displace the workforce in the implementation of specific tasks.[2]

In a broad sense, technological change is a permanent process in market economies. It is not only about the occasional discovery or invention of new technologies, but also about their dissemination and adoption across the economy and society, a process in which technologies are modified and improved through learning-by-doing and learning-by-using mechanisms.

In this context, it is extremely difficult to accurately quantify technological change. The most commonly used indicators are the efforts carried out in R&D and patents. However, these represent only partial and imperfect estimations. Measurements based on investment or staff working in R&D implicitly assume that there is a linear relationship between input and innovative results, ignoring other types of innovative activities of an informal, nonsystematic nature, which may also be relevant. Additionally, the use of representative surveys to gather statistical data does not capture people who may be developing high-impact innovations but are not included in the databases used to generate such statistics. (For example, when Steve Jobs was creating Apple in his garage, nobody asked him about his innovative activities.)

The indicator associated with the number of patents, in turn, assumes that the relevance and impact of all patents are the same. Some patent applications, however, are filed to block third-party innovative developments, or prevent or promote legal disputes, rather than to protect an innovation, and some patents protect innovations that never develop an economic use. Additionally, there are sectors that use other types of property rights,[3] and many important innovations are not patented but are protected using other means (such as secrecy) or are not protected legally but rather through "market" mechanisms (such as being the "first comer").

It could be argued that since technological progress should translate into productivity gains, the latter would be a proxy for the former. Nevertheless, productivity gains (even assuming they could be measured correctly, which is questionable, particularly when intangible assets are becoming increasingly important) may result from numerous causes other than technological change.

In short, the concept of technological change involves a variety of phenomena that cannot be subsumed under a single indicator or a limited number of variables, which inevitably will reflect only some of its dimensions, channels, or mechanisms. In fact, even a specific type of technological change, such as automation, may take a variety of shapes (mechanical robots, software robots, numerical control machines, CAD/CAM systems, or 3D print), making it difficult to have an empirically applicable homogeneous measure.

IMPACT OF AUTOMATION ON EMPLOYMENT DEMAND: SCALE EFFECT AND SUBSTITUTION EFFECT

A key idea in the literature is that technological change, especially automation, replaces human labor in the performance of tasks within occupations. Bresnahan (1999) and Autor, Levy, and Murnane (2003) provide evidence showing that new production technologies are frequently used to automate routine tasks, both cognitive and manual. These types of tasks are repetitive and follow an explicit set of rules that can be easily codified and run using computer software.

Automation may be considered a problem in situations in which machines would replace human work completely. For example, Frey and Osborne (2013) assessed 70 occupations to determine which could be "completely automated" using equipment controlled by state-of-the-art software. In collaboration with a group of researchers specialized in machine learning, they proposed in 2013 that, with current production technology, 37 occupations were susceptible to full automation, including accountants, auditors, bank loan agents, and mail carriers. Based on this analysis, the authors projected that nearly half of all jobs could be susceptible to full automation in the near future.

However, there is a relevant distinction that frequently leads to different diagnostics about the impact of technological change on the labor market. Following Bessen (2016), automating a task is not the same as automating an occupation. Occupations involve combinations of tasks that are performed by workers. New production technologies do not automate occupations; rather, they automate the tasks that may be specific to one occupation or used in different occupations. Therefore, automation may be partial (if only some tasks are automated) or full (if all tasks are automated). The economic difference between these concepts is important: Full automation implies a net loss of jobs; partial automation does not. In the 19th century, 98 percent of the labor required to weave a unit of cloth was automated, but the number of weaving jobs increased (Bessen 2016). The increased efficiency obtained through the incorporation of new production technologies resulted in lower final prices, which, due to the highly elastic demand, translated into an increased demand for textiles and, therefore, in a net increase of employment.

The paradigmatic example of this phenomenon today is the implementation and expansion of ATMs in U.S. commercial banks. ATMs can carry out most of the tasks performed by a bank employee. However, since the massive expansion of ATMs in the 1990s, the number of full-time bank employees has increased.[4] The use of ATMs, which lowered costs, encouraged the opening of new branches and, therefore, an increase in labor demand (Bessen 2016).

These examples suggest the importance of various dimensions within each market and value chain in the net effect on employment when new production technologies are introduced. The impact of technological change on employment may be different depending on the type of innovation involved and the relevant market structure. For example, product innovation could create employment through an increase in demand, but if the innovator has market power, its maximization strategy could lead to setting prices at levels that would imply a reduction of production (and, thus, of employment). Meanwhile, if the new product simply replaces other existing products and does not lead to changes in demand, employment would remain stable (De Elejalde, Giuliodori, and Stucchi 2015). Additionally, new products may be accompanied by process innovations that enable increased production efficiency and thus cancel or reduce the positive effects on employment (Calvino and Virgillito 2018). Another possibility is that companies that innovate in products or processes may displace other companies in the same market, which would lead to a decline in employment. If innovative companies are successful and expand, however, they will demand more from their suppliers, which could, in turn, grow and require more employment. Identifying and estimating these different sets of mechanisms would be intricate.

Another aspect that complicates empirical analysis in the case of automation is that, although the substitution effect occurs at the firm level, the scale effect may occur not only at that level but also downstream in the value chains (for example, clients may experience input cost reductions and thus expand their activity). The banking sector analysis in Bessen (2016) is an example of the first variant. In the dairy industry, automation of the milking process may produce a decrease in costs that can be transferred to milk-consuming sectors, resulting in an expansion of demand and an increase in scale and employment in companies producing cheese or other products.

Technological changes are altering the tasks that workers implement in their jobs, generating risks for some and opportunities for others. These changes will probably give better access to markets to individuals whose personal needs, restrictions, or preferences make traditional employment difficult. As these changes redefine and destroy some occupations, they also create new ones, such as opportunities for independent workers to interact through digital platforms and the possibility of providing goods and services that even 10 years ago didn't exist. In this sense, technological innovations in the workplace, such as industrial robots, may automate routine assembly line and light manufacturing jobs, which increases the risk of technological unemployment for some, but may also allow people with physical or cognitive limitations to participate in the labor market (Packard et al. 2019).

The literature on automation and employment is vast and based on different approaches. Acemoglu and Restrepo (2017) found negative effects of automation, as they recorded how the American regions most exposed to industrial automation suffered differential drops in employment and salaries between 1990 and 2007. In contrast, there are studies that find neutral or positive effects on the level of employment, with effects on workforce composition.

Among these, a study by Graetz and Michaels (2015) includes industrial automation data for 17 European countries between 1993 and 2007. These authors found that the adoption of robots had positive effects on labor productivity and wages, no impact on hours worked, and slightly biased labor demand toward high-skill jobs. (Graetz and Michaels [2015] compare national data, while Acemoglu and Restrepo [2017] use regional labor market data.[5])

Mann and Püttmann (2017) use as the explanatory variable of interest the number of U.S. patents somehow related to task automation. The authors found that the percentage of total patents related to automation grew from 25 percent to 67 percent between 1976 and 2014 (high figures reported may suggest that the method adopted leads to a wide definition of the concept of automation). In the paper, identified patents are associated with the industries in which they are likely to be used and, using data on sectoral employment structure, with local U.S. labor markets. The result is that automation improvements have positive effects on such markets: Although industrial employment declines, service sector labor significantly increases, offsetting the industrial sector losses. (In particular, there is a shift from industrial routine work to nonroutine work in the service sector.) Apella and Zunino (2017) obtained a similar outcome for Uruguay.

Autor and Salomons (2018) chose labor and total factor productivity as *proxy* variables. Their underlying logic is that, given the heterogeneity of innovation channels, it is preferable to use a variable that can be interpreted as the summary of their effects. Of course, this approach implies that the analysis is not only about automation, since other changes, such as product innovations or moving tasks offshore, may also have an impact on productivity. The research includes data for 19 countries—15 from the European Union, Australia, Japan, the Republic of Korea, and the United States—between 1970 and 2007. Their results show that productivity increases (particularly when using total factor productivity) have led to modest increases in employment, measured either as the total number of jobs or as labor force participation. These results are consistent with the "scale effects" arguments; even though the industries that experienced productivity gains destroyed employment, these losses were more than compensated for by the impact those gains generated in other activities, both by way of input-output links and through increases in final demand. By disaggregating the impact of productivity gains by sector, the authors found that gains in mining, utilities, and construction reduced employment because of their insignificant impact on other sectors, while manufacturing generated modest employment gains, and services slightly higher gains.

Other studies propose examining the relationship between the adoption of information and communication technology (ICT) and employment.[6] Michaels, Natraj, and van Reenen (2014) examined the impact of ICT investment on employment in 11 countries of the Organisation for Economic Co-operation and Development (OECD) between 1980 and 2004, finding that in industries with higher use of ICT, there is a displacement of medium-skilled workers in favor of high-skilled workers. Bessen (2016) found that the net effect of ICT use on employment is positive; employment grows significantly more in occupations that use such technologies, although part of the increase is at the expense of other occupations within the same industry. Moreover, the use of ICT generates loss of employment in low-wage jobs and gains in high-wage jobs and increases the share of workers with higher educational level. The use of computers is also associated with increasing wage inequality within occupations. In another study, Bessen (2017) found that the use of ICT is associated with increased employment in nonmanufacturing sectors and with a declining number of jobs in manufacturing sectors. This can be explained by the more elastic labor demand in the former versus higher demand satisfaction in the latter.

In a study of Argentina, Brambilla and Tortarolo (2018) found that the adoption of ICT leads to wage and productivity increases, particularly for high-productivity firms that employ high-skilled labor at the business level. In turn, such adoption induces a lower relative demand for low-skilled workers although, in absolute terms, it stimulates the creation of jobs in all skill categories (an effect more frequent in fast-growing companies).

Finally, Autor, Dorn, and Hanson (2015) discussed the relative impact of automation measured as the share of routine labor in overall employment in every U.S. regional labor market. Findings show, as expected, that automation does not have a significant impact on employment, although it does cause composition changes by reducing the share of routine tasks—both productive and administrative—in manufacturing and services, leading to wage polarization. Arntz, Gregory, and Zierahn (2016)—using a variable similar to that used by Autor, Dorn, and Hanson (2015) and working with European regions—found that the technological change that replaces routine tasks yields net gains in employment even if it replaces jobs, because cost savings encourage companies to increase their tradable goods demand, increasing employment in other sectors. Workers in those sectors then generate growing demand (and contribute to increasing employment) in nontradable sectors. Aaronson and Phelan (2018) examine the impact of minimum wage increases in the United States, assuming they tend to favor labor-saving technological changes. The authors found that such increases generate loss of employment in routine cognitive activities (such as those of bank tellers), have no impact on routine manual tasks, and generate positive effects on highly interpersonal activities (such as customer service).

It should be noted that all of the above-mentioned studies have limitations because data are not always fully available or reliable. Therefore, their results must be interpreted with caution. Studies based on firm surveys have been carried out in several countries for some time using standardized formats and a comprehensive coverage of innovative activities, but they rely on subjective answers. Hence, the results may be valid at the company level but overlook most aggregate effects.

Papers analyzing task automation are limited to specific forms of automation. Automation per se destroys jobs. However, the relevant question is that of the aggregate and long-term effects. Acemoglu and Restrepo (2017) found negative effects of automation on employment at the local market level, but these losses could be offset, either totally or partially, by employment gains in other areas. Additionally, studies using ICT data may be flawed; such technologies may replace human labor or they may complement it and, if so, increase the performance of workers mastering them.

IMPACT OF AUTOMATION ON EMPLOYMENT: POLARIZATION

Although the net effect of technical change on aggregate employment demand is not necessarily obvious, a change of profile can be expected. In this respect, technological change poses a risk for the labor market and its distributive impact. This discussion comes from the approach known as "task-biased technological change." According to this hypothesis, technological change tends to automate routine tasks that follow defined and specified procedures. These procedures can be compiled in a set of instructions and run using computer equipment. Autor, Katz, and Kearney (2008) proposed the hypothesis of task-biased technological change as an explanation for labor polarization, with employment concentrating in two main groups of workers: high-skilled, high-productivity, high-wage workers performing nonroutine cognitive-intensive tasks; and low-skilled workers relegated to nonroutine, manual-intensive tasks with low levels of productivity and wages. Mid-skilled and medium-wage workers, generally performing routine tasks (manual and cognitive), face lower demand for labor (Acemoglu and Autor 2011; Acemoglu 2002; Autor and Dorn 2009; Autor 2015). Figure 2.1 presents this phenomenon.

A decline in demand for routine tasks would increase, in relative terms, the demand for labor with higher concentrations of nonroutine cognitive tasks that require creativity, strong problem-solving, or interpersonal skills and nonroutine manual tasks that require situational adaptability, visual recognition, language use, and interpersonal skills. These two types of nonroutine skills lie at the opposite ends of the skill-income distribution: cognitive skills are usually performed by high-skilled workers, while manual tasks require a low level of qualification and, therefore, imply lower incomes.

Polarization can be observed in the occupational structure of the United States and Western Europe over the last three decades, with an increase in the share of both low- and high-skilled jobs (Goos and Manning 2007). Bussolo, Torre, and Winkler (2018) obtained similar results for Germany and Spain. Using harmonized data from the European Union Labor Force Survey, Goos, Manning, and Salomons (2008) found that in 14 of the 16 European countries for which there are available data, high-wage occupations grew compared to medium-wage occupations between 1990 and 2000, and in all 16 countries, low-wage occupations grew relative to medium-wage occupations.

According to the literature, labor force polarization is found mostly in developed countries. In emerging economies, there is a lower number of available jobs and evidence is not consistent with the results found for developed countries. In fact, Keister and Lewandowsky (2016) did not find evidence of labor polarization for Central and Eastern Europe; and Messina, Pica, and Oviedo (2016) did not find it for Latin America. In this group of countries, routine cognitive-intensive task employment requiring medium-skilled workers increased its share in overall employment. Maloney and Molina (2016) also found that only 2 of 21 developing countries analyzed show evidence of labor polarization.

FIGURE 2.1

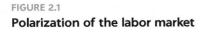

Polarization of the labor market

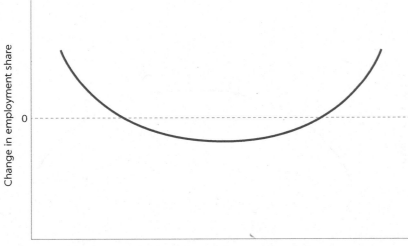

AGING OF TASKS

Polarization affects workers unequally; identifying the sociodemographic profiles of those in affected groups is important for understanding the phenomenon and proposing public policy responses. If innovations are adopted gradually, it would be reasonable to expect that the effects on different age groups would be diverse, so public policies should be designed to address this dimension. For example, if a new technology affects jobs usually offered to young people entering the labor market for the first time, policies should focus on ensuring that the educational system promotes skills for which demand is not declining. If the affected occupations are usually offered to young adults, policies should focus on helping them to upgrade and adapt their skills. Finally, in the case of adults near retirement age, it may be more effective to offer efficient social security programs that help them complete their work life and make an organized transition to retirement, instead of trying to update their working skills.

Autor and Dorn (2009) suggested the idea of aging in routine occupations. According to this hypothesis, young workers do not have incentives to enter occupations that are already contracting or, if already employed, to keep them. In addition, older workers, given the difficulties they face in upgrading their skills and reentering the labor market, have incentives to remain in such jobs, especially when they already have many years of experience. The outcome of these different incentives based on age ranges is known as task aging, with declining shares in the labor market (figure 2.2).

Public policies should be adjusted to recognize these effects if they are observed. If demand for certain skills is expected to gradually decline, a new cohort of workers should not focus on these skills but, instead, on others that might have higher demand, while those already working on tasks that demand these skills can continue doing so until retirement. In fact, if the tasks prevailing in some jobs are aging (for example, bus ticket seller), training programs should focus on young and middle-aged workers rather than on older individuals who will likely be able to continue working at the same jobs until retirement.

FIGURE 2.2

Aging of tasks

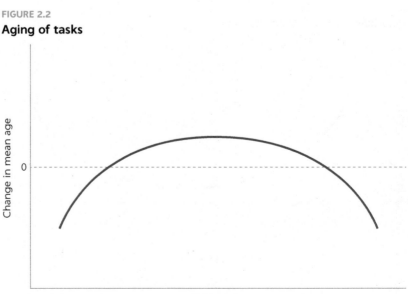

RELEVANT SKILLS AND SKILL ACQUISITION: WHAT AND WHEN?

Managing an effective education system to provide adequate skills to future workers is a critical challenge, as detailed information about future jobs is not necessarily available and providing specific technical training is problematic. The challenge, however, is to provide today's children and youth with the foundational skills, both cognitive and socioemotional, necessary to their ability to be creative, resilient, and cooperative and to adapt to an uncertain future.

The appropriate set of skills for employment is a credential that reduces the convergence of uncertainties in the transition from education to employment: Public-policy makers wonder which skills are most needed to achieve solid and sustainable productive development; youths worry about their futures and whether skill mismatches will expose them to high unemployment rates; educators wonder how to endow the young with such skills; and employers worry that new workers will not have the skills needed for their businesses. Research and debates are abundant, but the optimum combination of 21st-century skills required to effect permanent change and the most cost-effective strategies for promoting them are still open questions. However, the trends discussed in the previous subsection show that labor demand will likely concentrate in workers with the necessary skills to perform tasks with a high, nonroutine, cognitive content. Identifying these skills and how they are acquired is critical for the design of a development strategy for the coming decades.

An individual's skills are the abilities he or she may put into practice to satisfactorily solve a problem or carry out a task, whether simple or highly complex. In simple terms, a skill is the capacity of a person to do something well, because of a natural gift or as a result of training and practice (Schonfeld 2017). The skills spectrum is extremely broad, and ranges from the basic motor skills one learns at the earliest stages of life, through the strategic skills required to participate in classic children's games, to the complex combination of the skills necessary to solve advanced equations or write a screenplay.

A useful conceptualization of the skills needed for the 21st century comprises three broad categories: (1) foundational cognitive and socioemotional skills, (2) job-specific and technical skills (Arias and Bendini 2018), and (3) higher-order skills. The first category is related to knowledge acquisition and intelligence development. Foundational cognitive skills are mostly based on information processing, and are necessary to acquire intellectual, methodological, or specialized knowledge. Examples of these skills are memory and attention, and their development includes early mathematical skills, reading, and solving increasingly complex problems. Socioemotional skills refer to an individual's personality and are related to values, preferences, and emotions. Examples of socioemotional skills are the capacity to establish positive interpersonal relationships, communicate successfully, control oneself amid stressful situations, and work in teams.[7] Also, as pointed out by Arias and Bendini (2018), digital literacy (defined as "effective utilization of and interaction with ICT systems and devices") can be considered a foundational skill, as it implies a core capacity to work, communicate, and cooperate in increasingly digital environments.

Socioemotional skills complement cognitive skills, and both types constitute the basis for learning throughout an individual's lifetime.[8] For example, the ability to know and understand the rules of written communication is closely related to the ability to communicate successfully (Borghans et al. 2008). Socioemotional skills, though traditionally related to innate tendencies and early socialization (the best time to incorporate and develop socioeconomic skills being early childhood), can be acquired and strengthened throughout an individual's life. This observation is particularly relevant for the role that education systems, at their different stages, can play in training for the skills required for employment. Progress in the fields of psychology, neurobiology, and measurement instruments have shown that, far from being fixed and immutable, socioemotional skills can be learned in both formal and informal contexts and change as a consequence of important events in an individual's life. Even short interventions can produce significant results.[9]

A thorough review of the impact of socioemotional skills not only on the academic and employment paths, but also on aspects such as physical health, was conducted by Heckman and Kautz (2013); Heckman, Stixrud, and Urzúa (2006); and Heckman (2000). One of the best-known classifications of socioemotional skills is the Big-Five model, based on the gauge proposed by Goldberg (1993). This classification defines five categories based on the factor analysis of the answers given by individuals to questions concerning (1) openness, (2) conscientiousness, (3) agreeableness, (4) extraversion, and (5) neuroticism. Duckworth et al. (2007) broadened the conscientiousness dimension in their grit scale, a concept that groups a combination of self-confidence, passion, motivation, and persistence and which has earned an important place in educational theory. In a different approach, extraversion, conscientiousness, and openness have been positively related to employability by Wichert and Pohlmeier (2010), who noted that failing to consider socioemotional skills in employment background would lead to overestimating the effects of formal educational assets.

This wide diversity of findings suggests that there is no obvious option for educational public policy makers, but offers some general principles that should guide their actions:

- produce better evidence in the specific context of each education system to pinpoint strengths and weaknesses in skill assets;
- training in specific technical skills, which are permanently at risk of becoming outdated, should at all times be accompanied by long-term training in foundational cognitive and socioemotional skills; the time invested in technical aspects should be limited or, if possible, allocated to employers' investment.

The socioemotional skills area is relatively new in educational literature. The debate is far from being closed, many of its taxonomies and measuring attempts still overlap, and there are no definitive conceptualizations. However, many empirical studies prove that, controlling for the effects of traditionally measured indicators (years of formal schooling or performance in cognitive areas), socioemotional skills *do* explain the success in individuals' educational paths. Variables such as openness, willingness to engage in teamwork, and self-confidence are the emotional bases on which cognitive and technical learning become more sustainable and underpin human capital's capacity for constant adaptation, which brings about an elective affinity for technological change. Even more interestingly, intervention experiences in this field suggest that short, specific, and low-cost interventions can lead to significant improvement, and, contrary to traditional assumptions, these skills are not fixed and determined only in the first stages of life but are susceptible of training and change at different times along the educational path.

The second broad category is that of job-specific and technical skills. These skills might be very specific to a sector of activity, profession, market, or even to one particular firm. Some technical skills might require a prior endowment or some complex cognitive and socioemotional traits, but too-specific skills that are typically required to perform routine and simpler tasks are more at risk of being replaced by automation. This is relevant because public policy concerning the acquisition of labor skills usually resorts to narrow technical skill reconversion programs or too-specific task training courses (Cunningham and Villaseñor 2016); these types of technical training usually produce neutral or even negative returns. Moreover, even though the conventional wisdom in public policy discourse stresses the importance of "teaching trades," the available evidence suggests that technical skills are in less demand by employers. Often, policies that seek to facilitate workers' labor reconversion focus more on the possibilities provided at educational establishments (such as available specialists, or institutional traditions and logics) than on labor market demand.

Narrow technical skills are those less correlated with the development of nonroutine cognitive tasks. Using the O*NET database,[10] which identifies for each occupation a set of related characteristics, it is possible to link occupations to the tasks carried out by workers and, subsequently, with the skills needed to develop such tasks. Figure 2.3 shows a positive and significant correlation between cognitive and socioemotional skills and the performance of nonroutine cognitive tasks.

FIGURE 2.3

Correlation between nonroutine cognitive tasks and necessary skills

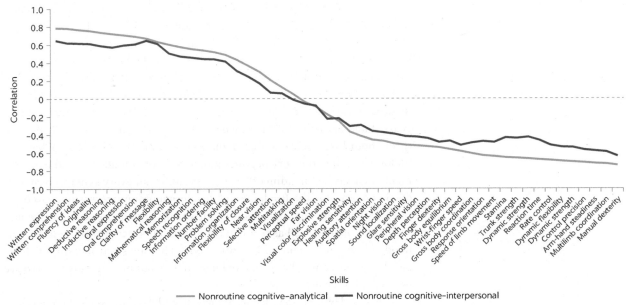

Source: World Bank calculations based on O*NET 24.1 (database), O*NET OnLine (accessed November 2018), www.onetonline.org.

Finally, higher-order skills are most likely to be required in periods of rapid technological change. These skills are needed to adapt to uncertainty and constant change because they involve critical thinking, complex problem solving, and the capacity for permanent learning. As higher-order skills build on robust foundations of cognitive, socioemotional, and relevant technical skills, workers who can apply higher-order skills will solve complex and unexpected problems and thus be the less likely to be replaced by the automation of tasks using robots and algorithms (see box 2.1).

Different skills are acquired at different ages and in different contexts. With respect to investment in human capital, the encouragement and conditions for skills development are found throughout the stages of life (early childhood and childhood, adolescence and youth, and adult life), and each of these stages relates to one public-policy area, for example, early childhood education and support for young families with small children (school and home), the different mandatory and higher schooling levels (primary, secondary, technical, and university education), and professional education on the job, linked to the concept of lifelong learning. In all these stages and areas, investment in human capital education will be a combination of public and private spending.

Support for public investment in these fields ranges from the most traditional, such as school infrastructure and teacher hiring and training, to the support of family care systems (for example, childcare systems that both complement and reinforce parents' roles in the training of basic cognitive and socioemotional literacy, and allow time for mothers to return to work), through professional training programs that offer reconversion tools amid the entry of new technologies in specific sectors. However, even though skills can be acquired and strengthened throughout life, different types of skills can be more efficiently learned at different stages. A relevant role of policy makers is to design educational and training skills that target future and current workers, providing opportunities to develop skills in the most fruitful ages and periods of academic and labor cycles.

The effectiveness of investment in different types of skills will vary depending on which part of the life cycle it is intended to affect (Arias and Bendini (2018, § 2.2); Filgueira and Porzecanski (2017, § 1.c). During the early years (children from birth to 3–4 years, and even before birth), the most critical developments take place in the brain, setting the foundation for all learning processes and higher-order skills development that occur later in life. Although brain plasticity never ends throughout an individual's life, it is at its peak in early childhood. The consequences of deprivation during these years (such as malnourishment or lack of qualified care) might endure throughout life. Early emotional and physical health are the very basis of lifelong learning, the very beginning of a cycle of cumulative skill development. As Arias and Bendini (2018, 6) point out, "not every skill can be developed at every age; the fundamental developmental processes need to be in place [at] the optimal periods for cultivating higher-order cognitive and socioemotional, as well as technical and ICT skills, occur throughout childhood, adolescence, and early adulthood." This does not mean that those developments cannot be stimulated later in life, but investments to do so are markedly less cost-effective.

The period between 5 years of age and early adolescence is ideal for developing basic numeracy and literacy, and memory and social skills, as well as possibly correcting for previous weaknesses in the formation of foundational skills.

BOX 2.1

Measuring problem solving: A skill for the 21st century

Complex problem solving or collaborative problem solving (CPS), one of the skills considered crucial for the 21st century, is defined as the capacity of an individual, either in isolation or as part of a team, to solve a problem for which there is no predefined routine method. The solution process requires multiple skills: cognitive (such as the capacity to infer and systematize information), emotional (such as creativity and critical thought), the simultaneous handling of different types of knowledge (such as numerical and linguistic), and, in the case of CPS, social skills (communication and a cooperative attitude) (Greiff, Holt, and Funke 2013; OECD 2013).

Complex problem solving as a challenge for educational systems has created an important knowledge and research field; learning this skill requires not only that schools broaden teaching beyond curricular content but also that they maximize the flow of social skills learned by the young outside school. As noted by Csapó and Funke (2017), it is not possible to properly encourage the development of this complex skill combination in ad hoc courses, and the most promising experiences have been curriculum-based interventions, often with the help of technological solutions (such as adaptive learning platforms, gamification, and online games).

The Program for International Student Assessment (PISA) measures this skill regardless of the traditional areas and, since 2015, has been administering the cooperative problem-solving assessment in a computer-based format. This assessment focuses on the skills required to (1) identify problems whose solution calls for skills from multiple subject areas, (2) identify the available information and restrictions, (3) represent the possible alternatives and solution paths and select the strategies to solve the problem, (4) check the solutions or think about them, and (5) communicate the results. The cooperative dimension assesses the skills to generate and maintain comprehension collectively, agree on the actions to be carried out, and establish and maintain team organization.

One of the most relevant conclusions reached from the PISA results in the problem-solving area is that, after the effects of the cognitive variables in problem-solving have been removed (that is, after controlling for the results obtained by each student in science, reading, and mathematics), the socioeconomic differences among students were not significant. This suggests that less favorable home and social environments, typically assumed to be less capable of reinforcing and supplementing traditional cognitive ability in young people, are able to underpin and reinforce other skills related to sociability, the appreciation for collaboration, and cooperation between peers (OECD 2017). Thus, interventions for the development of problem-solving skills could become an effective path to increasing inclusion and educational equality.

Why should an educational system intervene in the CPS field? Success in an employment market that is characterized by accelerated change is rooted in the ability to solve complex problems. A study of the job markets in seven countries has shown that an increase of 1 standard deviation in complex problem-solving skills is associated with 10 to 20 percent higher wages (World Bank 2019). The complex problem-solving field contributes to the very foundations of the two dimensions of educational quality: (1) cognitive development and (2) the socioemotional and higher-order skills required to upgrade knowledge and process information on an ongoing basis. In addition, training in these skills could be optimized in different areas of school activity, maximizing opportunities to motivate the young. Aggregate data show that participating in physical education lessons correlates with better attitudes toward collaboration and teamwork. Moreover, the best performance in this area is positively related to positive school climate indicators; for example, after controlling for the effects of cognitive performance, students who believe they have been treated fairly by their teachers obtain the best results (OECD 2017). These findings suggest that teachers and schools have several options for proposing activities to develop new skills and finding opportunities to work cooperatively in different areas and subjects, maximizing the possibilities offered by the technological tools to practice practical problem solving: "In an increasingly virtual world, perhaps today's children are inadvertently training themselves to become better collaborative problem solvers simply by going on line" (OECD 2017, 66).

Later in adolescence and toward youth, cognitive and social skills become more stable, and openness to education enables more specialized learning: although higher-order skills continue developing, technical skills are best developed during early youth (Filgueira and Porzecanski 2017).

Based on the affinities between life stages and opportunities to learn skills, some basic policies can be formulated (Arias and Bendini 2018). First, foundational cognitive and socioemotional skills should be available for everyone in a fair, democratic, and inclusive society. A dramatic improvement in the quality of basic education, ensuring robust literacy and numeracy skills, will enable the subsequent development of adequate higher-order ICT and complex technical skills for the workforce of the future.

Second, remedial education and workplace and other types of nonformal training should be offered to active workers; maintaining market relevance and quality assurance systems improve inclusion and equity for adults. It is important to incentivize both employers and workers in the process, so that the former increase the supply of relevant training services, and the latter have access to enough information to make informed decisions. Also, science, technology, engineering, and mathematics (STEM) education, which has been shown to increase productivity and boost human capital, should be promoted through active incentive policies.

Finally, wise use of new technology in education can produce dramatic improvements in human capital. For instance, adaptive learning software enables student-centered customized education, providing feedback, learning support, and constant self-evaluation and adaptation of inputs and difficulty levels (see box 2.2). Project-based education through robotics is another successful strategy for boosting higher-order skills development for children and adolescents. Some promising experiences have already been launched in Uruguayan schools, and the relevant policy implications are discussed in the subsection "Encouraging Skills for the Job of the Future" in chapter 4.

BOX 2.2

PAM: A successful experience of adaptive learning in Uruguayan schools

The Adaptive Platform for Mathematics (PAM), launched by Plan Ceibal in 2013, supports mathematics learning, teaching, and exercises. PAM reached 51,000 children in 2013 and 129,000 users in 2016. A quantitative evaluation of the impact of PAM was carried out by a team of researchers from the Research, Evaluation and Statistic Division (DIEE) (the statistics and research agency of the National Administration of Public Education, ANEP) and Center of Economic Research (CINVE), an independent economics institute.[a] The research showed that:

- PAM has a positive significant impact on learning outcomes for all students;
- progress in learning outcomes is systematically higher for users than for nonusers; and
- learning progress was higher for more disadvantaged students.

The use of PAM in class, requiring teamwork and teacher guidance, showed better outcomes than its use by individual students, suggesting the importance of teacher training for the use of adaptative learning technologies.

a. Plan Ceibal, "The Effect of PAM on Math Learning." https://www.ceibal.edu.uy/es/articulo/el-efecto-de-pam-en-el-aprendizaje-de -matematica.

THE ROLE OF LABOR AND SOCIAL SECURITY REGULATIONS

The discussion so far has focused on how technological changes affect labor supply and demand, and the role of skills in labor markets. Also relevant are the interactions between innovation-induced labor market changes and labor regulations and social security. New technologies may affect how workers relate to employers or customers and how these changes affect social security systems.

Most of the literature in this area focuses on the role of the new forms of employment created by new technology. Specifically, the discussion centers around the "gig economy,"[11] the advantages and risks that this new model introduces to the economy and workers, and how existing institutions should adjust to take advantage of opportunities and limit potential negative consequences.

Technological innovations, through digital technology and the internet, enabled the development of new business models that facilitated contacts between suppliers and consumers, thus reducing transactional costs and market friction. These models include the gig economy, which has raised the interest of policy makers and researchers. The gig economy includes at least two new forms of industrial organization: crowdwork and on-demand work, which are usually managed through platforms running on mobile applications (De Stefano 2016). Crowdwork refers to the production of services through a series of independent activities that are integrated through an online platform. These platforms connect multiple individuals through the internet, allowing collaboration at a global level. On-demand work is a form of employment under which the execution of certain activities, such as transportation and delivery of goods, is organized through a web or mobile application.

These new forms of employment may offer access to more flexible and autonomous jobs, increase personal efficiency and skills, and result in a better work life–personal life balance (Valenduc and Vendramin 2016; Degryse 2016). Likewise, the possibility of working from home and on a flexible schedule makes work more compatible with other duties, such as taking care of family members or managing health conditions, that preclude workers from going to a workplace (Berg 2016). Other potential advantages of these new forms of employment include facilitating independent workers' access to a broader market through the internet or using some assets, such as cars, more efficiently (De Stefano 2016).

Firms may also benefit from access to thousands of workers available to complete specific activities in a short time, with no company-worker obligations or costs of setting up an office (Berg et al. 2018). This model also offers the possibility of extending the network of providers and clients, increasing scale and benefits (World Bank 2019). However, these potential benefits may be offset by negative effects, such as a weakening of labor regulations, as labor markets become based on completion of tasks instead of employment. Other aspects of modern capitalist societies—such as access to social security, availability of dispute resolution systems for labor relations, and a clear distinction between work and leisure time—may also be at risk, and traditional (even if imperfect) solutions to problems such as information asymmetry in labor relations may be lost (Valenduc and Vendramin 2016; Degryse 2016). Nevertheless, technological change is generating economic activity that will need to be addressed by labor regulations. As these activities become more prevalent, policy makers will need to acknowledge them, and the relative size of the informal economy and employment should decline (Packard et al. 2019).

Estimating the reach of work in the gig economy is difficult. First, there is no clear definition for this sector, and different authors use different criteria; second, the nature of these activities is continuously changing due to the introduction of new technological innovations, so that definitions and measurement criteria that seem reasonable one day may quickly become obsolete; and third, access to reliable sources of information is limited (Forde et al. 2017). However, there is general agreement that these practices have increased exponentially since 2007–08, after the international financial crisis (Huws et al. 2017).

Data gathered from big companies that administer and manage platforms show that platforms include about eight million workers at the global level (Smith and Leberstein 2015). About 1.3 million individuals (4 percent of the working population) in the United Kingdom are estimated to be working in the gig economy, and this number is increasing (CIPD 2017). Research carried out in seven European countries revealed that between 9 percent and 22 percent of the population completed some type of virtual job through a platform (Huws et al. 2017). In Latin America, there are not yet enough data to measure this phenomenon, but indirect estimates indicate that its adoption has been slower than in more developed countries, with transportation and delivery applications at the forefront, surpassing crowdworking platforms (Beccaria and Maurizio 2019).

Even though the gig economy is considered an innovation, its expansion seems to be part of a wider trend of nonstandard forms of employment, defined as labor arrangements that deviate from the traditional full-time wage earner model that has prevailed in developed economies in recent times.

Discussions about the impact of new technology on labor relationships and social security may be analyzed in three different dimensions: (1) the areas in which these new forms of employment have gained relevance; (2) the profiles of workers participating in these new arrangements, which will enable an understanding of their needs and opportunities; and (3) based on the first two dimensions, the impact these new forms of employment may have on labor relationships.

Defining crowdwork and on-demand work through web applications

The gig economy phenomenon embraces two types of online platform: crowdwork and on-demand work, both using a mobile application. In Latin America, on-demand work seems to be more widely accepted, mainly in transportation and delivery applications.

These platforms share the common feature of administering a workforce through an algorithm (Berg et al. 2018). Algorithms have been used in the past to organize production processes; on the new digital platforms, however, algorithms not only assign tasks but control every aspect of the job, including monitoring employees' behavior and performance. Employees interact with the platform instead of with other individuals, in many cases with no knowledge of the rules that govern the algorithm, which may change as new information is gathered (Möhlmann and Zalmanson 2017).

Crowdwork is a form of production carried out through online platforms that allow multiple organizations and individuals to connect through the internet, to make specific contributions, or supply services or goods. These platforms operate as a virtual market for microtasks in different industries, such as webpages or software development; design, image, and video recognition; data gathering; translations; or audio transcription or database analysis (Valenduc and Vendramin 2016). Some of the most prominent platforms are Amazon Mechanical Turk, CrowdFlower, Clickworker, Microworkers, and Prolific. Crowdwork platforms provide companies access to a large number of flexible workers spread around the world for the quick completion of small tasks that contribute to the production of a final product. All the activities can be carried out remotely using a computer (Berg et al. 2018).

On-demand work is characterized by the establishment of a noncontinuous employment relationship. An employer agrees to contact an employee when and if work is required but with no commitment to do so (Valenduc and Vendramin 2016). This model is similar to that traditionally used by temporary employment agencies, but much more flexible and at a larger scale. The traditional intermediation provided by temporary agencies is now managed by an algorithm. Thus, the platforms that manage on-demand work offer a combination of a communication tool and an algorithm to efficiently connect customers and workers registered in the system. The platform is also used to define and monitor quality of service, as well as to select and manage the workforce (De Stefano 2016). Among the most important platforms in Latin America are Uber, for transportation; and Pedidos Ya, Glovo, Rappi, and SoyDelivery, for delivery services.

Unlike crowdwork, which can draw on employees all over the world, on-demand work can only be carried out locally, creating a geographic connection between customers and workers. Furthermore, in crowdwork platforms there may be no personal contact between the client and the service provider, while in on-demand work through a platform such contact exists by design.

Profiling the population working in the gig economy

The number of participants in the gig economy is very difficult to establish. In addition to the definition and methodological issues already discussed, participants may work full or part time, or may register but never accept a job (Forde et al. 2017). However, the apparent rapid growth of this sector has led researchers to investigate the profiles of individuals working through these platforms, their employment conditions, how much they are paid, and how much access they have to social protection. In the last few years several surveys to characterize this population have been carried out (e.g., Berg 2016; Berg et al. 2018; Forde et al. 2017; and Huws et al. 2017). These surveys have been developed to provide evidence and information and to validate the assumptions related to the benefits and risks that these new forms of organization of work provide.

Among the most interesting findings in these surveys (mostly carried out in developed countries), the population engaged in crowdwork platform work seems to be relatively young, mostly under 40 years old. More men than women participate in crowdworking, and they are usually well educated, with more than 80 percent holding some type of technical or university degree, according to one of the surveys. Most participants chose to join the platforms to supplement income received from their main occupation. In some cases—32 percent, according to Berg et al. (2016) and 25 percent, according to the European Parliament (Huws et al. 2017)—participation in crowdwork is the worker's main source of income and, while pleased by the possibility of setting their work schedules, workers are concerned about employment continuity, financial protection in the case of health problems, and financial instability.

Labor regulation implications

Although the gig economy introduced some innovations to labor markets, employment relations are, in many respects, similar to those already existing in independent and informal markets. For example, crowdwork could be considered to be a step in Taylorism, because it splits production into multiple activities assigned to individual workers, but at a scale significantly greater than Frederick Taylor envisioned in the 1880s and with some managers' roles, such as allocating of activities across the labor force and monitoring performance, now implemented by algorithms. Similarly, temporary employment agencies used to provide a service similar to that of on-demand platforms (Berg et al. 2018). For example, Uber provides one of the strongest innovations in the automation of administration, by organizing the availability of a driver in time and space when requested.

Some authors have expressed concerns about the risk of the gig economy becoming a new source of low-quality jobs, without adequate labor or social protection (Bensusán 2016; Berg 2016; Cherry 2016; De Stefano 2016). Platforms present themselves as a contact facilitator between independent workers and prospective clients but do not acknowledge a labor relationship with those offering their skills through them. Thus, the companies that manage the platforms do not assume the legal obligations of a typical employment relationship, such as the right to a minimum wage or overtime, making contributions to the social security system, or ensuring a safe and healthy working environment.

This approach has been challenged legally in some countries. For example, in the United States, legal actions brought by Uber drivers demanding the minimum wage and payment for overtime hours have gained momentum, and other actions against several on-demand work or crowdwork platforms have been filed as well (Cherry 2016).[12] In Argentina, workers using platforms such as Pedidos Ya, Rappi, and Glovo are organizing a union, and Uber drivers have recently called for a global strike to demand higher rates and job security.

The arguments in favor of the freelance relationship include ones that workers may decide their own hours, connect or disconnect the application at will, and have the power to reject a job, which employees under traditional employment relationships cannot. Likewise, platform workers use and control their own working tools, such as telephones, computers, equipment, and internet connections.

The arguments rejecting independence in the relationship include ones that platforms' control over workers is greater than it may seem because customer assessment systems give them control over workers' performance, that platforms provide training and some tools, and that platforms establish basic rules for the services delivered that, if not satisfied, may result in platforms' reducing or eliminating the offer of gigs to workers.

The debate regarding the legal status of gig economy workers is far from over; discussions and litigation continue in various countries to decide whether these workers are employees of digital platforms or independent workers that sell services in the market (Cherry 2016; De Stefano 2016). The legal debate over how to classify gig economy workers using the existing employment categories is probably masking a more relevant discussion—whether the existing categories are adequate to regulate these jobs or whether a new model—which acknowledges the independent nature of these activities but, at the same time, provides basic protections against social risks (unemployment, sickness, old age, and working accidents) and protects essential labor rights—is needed.

Insufficient labor and social protection are by no means issues exclusive to the gig economy, but the emergence of this new model of employment is creating serious challenges for policy makers, who may need to adopt new regulations. Some of the problems are similar to those of traditional nonstandard forms of employment, which include temporary jobs, part-time or on-demand jobs, working for temporary employment agencies or as a subcontracted worker, and the disguised employment or self-employment relationship (ILO 2016). Therefore, the discussion of how to create safer and more decent forms of employment within the gig economy should probably be part of a larger debate about labor market regulation (De Stefano 2016).

This is a particular concern in Europe, where, between 2007 and 2015, nonstandard forms of employment increased. Part-time employment went from 17.5 percent to 19.6 percent of the labor force, and temporary employment increased in 23 out of 33 countries (Spasova et al. 2017). The situation is different in Latin America, where nonstandard employment has always been high. Informality and insufficient access to social security have been common in most countries (World Bank 2019). With some cyclical variations, nonstandard employment incidence in Latin America has barely changed in the last two decades. Most countries evidence similar distributions to those in the mid-2010s and the 1990s. Brazil and Uruguay, however, had a decrease of about 10 and 5 percent, respectively, and Mexico saw an increase of 5 percent (Apella and Zunino 2018). The level of education and income for workers in nonstandard forms of employment showed increases in some countries, but not in all (Apella and Zunino 2018).

Finally, the growth of platforms in Latin America may enable the formalization of the informal economy, as better information is collected and centralized. Platform workers register in the system, and most financial transactions are done through formal electronic channels, in contrast to the traditional informal work that is unregistered and mostly cash-based (Beccaria and Maurizio 2019; Huws 2019). Whether the growth of platforms is large enough to affect the informal economy depends on how fast (and far) they grow, and whether regulations facilitate them or force them back into informal channels.

NOTES

1. In practice, different types of innovations usually complement each other; for example, the introduction of a new product may require changes in processes or marketing methods, and a process innovation may induce changes in the way work is organized.
2. For robot manufacturers, the introduction of new or improved robots represents a product innovation, while for their users it represents a process innovation.
3. In the case of agriculture, for instance, there is a system designed to protect new varieties of plants resulting from agreements made in the International Union for the Protection of New Varieties of Plants (UPOV), which is widely used around the world.

4. Between 1999 and 2009, 200,000 ATMs were deployed in the U.S. financial sector, while the demand for bank tellers increased at a 2 percent annual rate.

5. Although Acemoglu and Retrepo rely on data on penetration of robots at the regional level, they estimate automation by combining the weighted robot adoption level by sector and industrial structure in each region.

6. See Dutz, Almeida, and Packard (2018) for a discussion and an analytical model on the possible effects on employment of using ICT.

7. See Almlund et al. (2011) for an extensive review of how the literature has classified different types of skills, especially with respect to the possibility of measuring for use as explanatory variables.

8. The term "noncognitive skills" is often used in contrast to the skills classically taught in educational environments (writing, reading comprehension, and solving mathematical operations), but all skills are cognitive because they all involve brain functions.

9. See especially Durlak et al. (2011); see also Cook et al. (2014); Heckman and Kautz (2013); and Chernyshenko, Kankaraš, and Drasgow (2018) for reviews of interventions with significant effects in dimensions such as school climate, academic predisposition, and criminal behavior.

10. O*NET (Occupational Information Network) provides information on the content of occupational tasks. Since 2003, O*NET has been compiled in the United States for approximately 1,000 occupations based on the Standard Occupational Classification (SOC) and updated periodically through 2019. See O*NET 24.1 (database), O*NET OnLine (accessed November 2018), www.onetonline.org.

11. The term "gig" refers to a single performance by a stage artist, such as a musician or comedian. "Gig economy" has been adopted to define a way of working that consists of a succession of individual jobs.

12. Cherry (2016) analyzes 14 legal actions filed by workers of several on-demand work or crowdwork platforms in the United States.

REFERENCES

Aaronson, D., and B. Phelan. 2018. "The Potential to Automate Low-Wage Jobs in the U.S. and Its Impact on Workers." London School of Economics U.S. Centre (blog), August 11. http://bit.ly/2KI74ww.

Acemoglu, D. 2002. "Technical Change, Inequality, and the Labor Market." *Journal of Economic Literature* 40 (1): 7–72. https://economics.mit.edu/files/4124.

Acemoglu, D., and D. Autor. 2011. "Skills, Tasks and Technologies: Implications for Employment and Earning." In *Handbook of Labor Economics*, vol. 4, edited by O. Ashenfelter and D.E. Card, 1043–1171. Amsterdam: Elsevier.

Acemoglu, D., and P. Restrepo. 2017. "Robots and Jobs: Evidence from U.S. Labor Markets." NBER Working Paper 23285, National Bureau of Economic Research, Cambridge, MA: https://www.nber.org/papers/w23285.pdf.

Almlund, M., A. L. Duckworth, J. Heckman, and T. Kautz. 2011. "Personality Psychology and Economics." In *Handbook of the Economics of Education*, edited by E. A. Hanushek, S. Machin, and L. Woessmann, 1–181. Amsterdam: Elsevier.

Apella, I., and G. Zunino. 2017. "Technological Change and the Labor Market in Argentina and Uruguay. A Task Content Analysis." Policy Research Working Paper 8215, World Bank, Washington, DC. https://openknowledge.worldbank.org/handle/10986/28550.

Apella, I., and G. Zunino. 2018. "Nonstandard Forms of Employment in Developing Countries: A Study for a Set of Selected Countries in Latin America and the Caribbean and Europe and Central Asia." Policy Research Working Paper 8581, World Bank, Washington DC. https://openknowledge.worldbank.org/handle/10986/30426.

Arias, O., and M. Bendini. 2018. *Building Skills for the Future World of Work*. World Bank, Washington, DC.

Arntz, M., T. Gregory, and U. Zierahn. 2016. "The Risk of Automation for Jobs in OECD Countries: A Comparative Analysis." OECD Social, Employment and Migration Working Papers 189, OECD, Paris. https://www.ifuturo.org/sites/default/files/docs/automation.pdf.

Autor, D. 2015. "Why Are There Still So Many Jobs? The History and Future of Workplace Automation." *Journal of Economic Perspectives* 29 (3): 3–30. https://economics.mit.edu /files/11563.

Autor, D., and D. Dorn. 2009. "This Job Is Getting Old: Measuring Changes in Job Opportunities Using Occupational Age Structure." *American Economic Review: Papers & Proceedings* 99 (2): 45–51.

Autor, D., D. Dorn, and G. Hanson. 2015. "Untangling Trade and Technology: Evidence from Local Labour Markets." *Economic Journal* 125 (584): 621–46. https://economics.mit.edu/files/11564.

Autor, D., F. L. Katz, and M. S. Kearney. 2008. "Trends in U.S. Wage Inequality: Revising the Revisionists." *Review of Economics and Statistics* 90 (2): 300–23. https://economics.mit.edu /files/586.

Autor, D., F. Levy, and R. Murnane. 2003. "The Skill Content of Recent Technological Change: An Empirical Exploration." *Quarterly Journal of Economics* 118 (4): 1279–1333. https:// economics.mit.edu/files/11574.

Autor, D., and A. Salomons. 2018. "Is Automation Labor-Displacing? Productivity Growth, Employment and the Labor Share." NBER Working Paper 24871, National Bureau of Economic Research, Cambridge, MA. https://www.nber.org/papers/w24871.pdf.

Beccaria, L., and R. Maurizio. 2019. "Algunas-reflexiones-en-torno-al-empleo-en-plataformas -y-a-los-mecanismos-de-proteccion." *Alquimias Económicas*, February 27. https:// alquimiaseconomicas.com/2019/02/27/algunas-reflexiones-en-torno-al-empleo-en -plataformas-y-a-los-mecanismos-de-proteccion/.

Bensusán, G. 2016. *New Employment Trends: Challenges and Options for Labor Market Policies and Regulations*. Santiago, Chile: Economic Commission for Latin America and the Caribbean.

Berg, J., 2016. "Income Security in the On-Demand Economy: Findings and Policy Lessons from a Survey of Crowdworkers." Conditions of Work and Employment Series 74, International Labour Organization, Geneva. https://www.ilo.org/wcmsp5/groups/public/---ed_protect /---protrav/---travail/documents/publication/wcms_479693.pdf.

Berg, J., M. Furrer, E. Harmon, U. Rani, and M. S. Silberman. 2018. *Digital Labour Platforms and the Future of Work: Towards Decent Work in the Online World*. Geneva: International Labour Organization. https://www.ilo.org/wcmsp5/groups/public/---dgreports/---dcomm/--- publ/documents/publication/wcms_645337.pdf.

Bessen, J. 2016. "How Computer Automation Affects Occupations: Technology, Jobs, and Skills." Law and Economics Research Paper 15-49, Boston University School of Law, Boston. https://ssrn.com/abstract=2690435.

Bessen, J. 2017. "Automation and Jobs: When Technology Boosts Employment." Law and Economics Research Paper 17-09, Boston University School of Law, Boston. https:// ssrn.com/abstract=2935003.

Borghans, L., A. L. Duckworth, J. J. Heckman, and B. Ter Weel. 2008. "The Economics and Psychology of Personality Traits." *Journal of Human Resources* 43 (4): 972–1059.

Brambilla, I., and D. Tortarolo. 2018. "Investment in ICT, Productivity, and Labor Demand: The Case of Argentina." Policy Research Working Paper 8325, World Bank, Washington, DC. https://openknowledge.worldbank.org/handle/10986/29290.

Bresnahan, T. 1999. "Computerisation and Wage Dispersion: An Analytic Reinterpretation." *Economic Journal* 109 (456): 390–415.

Bussolo, M., I. Torre, and H. Winkler. 2018. "Accounting for the Role of Occupational Change on Earnings in Europe and Central Asia." IZA Conference Working Paper. http://conference .iza.org/conference_files/WoLabConf_2018/torre_i26373.pdf.

Calvino, F., and M. Virgillito. 2018. "The Innovation-Employment Nexus: A Critical Survey of Theory and Empirics." *Journal of Economic Surveys* 32 (1): 83–117.

Chernyshenko, O., M. Kankaraš, and F. Drasgow. 2018. "Social and Emotional Skills for Student Success and Wellbeing: Conceptual Framework for the OECD Study on Social and Emotional Skills." OECD Education Working Paper 173. OECD, Paris.

Cherry, M. 2016. "Beyond Misclassification: The Digital Transformation of Work." *Comparative Labor Law & Policy Journal* 37 (3): 544–77.

CIPD (Chartered Institute of Personnel and Development). 2017. *To Gig or Not to Gig? Stories from the Modern Economy*. Dublin: CIPD.

Cook, P. J., K. Dodge, G. Farkas, R. G. Fryer Jr., J. Guryan, J. Ludwig, S. Mayer, H. Pollack, and L. Steinberg. 2014. "The (Surprising) Efficacy of Academic and Behavioral Intervention with Disadvantaged Youth: Results from a Randomized Experiment in Chicago." NBER Working Paper 19862, National Bureau of Economic Research, Cambridge, MA. https://www.nber.org/papers/w19862.pdf.

Csapó, B., and J. Funke. 2017. "The Development and Assessment of Problem Solving in 21st Century Schools." In *The Nature of Problem Solving: Using Research to Inspire 21st Century Learning*, edited by B. Csapó and J. Funke, 19–32. Paris: OECD. https://doi.org/10.1787/9789264273955-3-en.

Cunningham, W., and P. Villaseñor. 2016. "Employer Voices, Employer Demands, and Implications for Public Skills Development Policy." Policy Research Working Paper 7582, World Bank, Washington, DC. https://openknowledge.worldbank.org/handle/10986/23921.

Evangelista, R., and A. Vezzani. 2012. "The Impact of Technological and Organizational Innovations in Employment in European Firms." *Industrial and Corporate Change* 21 (4): 871–99.

De Elejalde, R., D. Giuliodori, and R. Stucchi. 2015. "Employment and Innovation: Firm-Level Evidence from Argentina." *Emerging Markets Finance and Trade* 51 (1): 27–47. http://fen.uahurtado.cl/wp-content/uploads/2010/07/I-291.pdf.

De Stefano, V., 2016. "The Rise of the 'Just-in-Time Workforce': On-Demand Work, Crowd Work and Labour Protection in the 'Gig-Economy.'" Conditions of Work and Employment Series 71, International Labour Organization, Geneva. https://www.ilo.org/wcmsp5/groups/public/---ed_protect/---protrav/---travail/documents/publication/wcms_443267.pdf.

Degryse, C. 2016. "Digitalisation of the Economy and Its Impact on Labour Markets." Working Paper 2016.03, European Trade Union Institute, Brussels. https://papers.ssrn.com/sol3/papers.cfm?abstract_id=2730550.

Duckworth, A., C. Peterson, M. Matthews, and D. Kelly. 2007. "Grit: Perseverance and Passion for Long Term Goals." *Journal of Personality and Social Psychology* 92 (6): 1087–1101.

Durlak, J., R. Weissberg, A. Dymnicki, R. Taylor, and K. Schellinger. 2011. "The Impact of Enhancing Students' Social and Emotional Learning: A Meta-Analysis of School-Based Universal Interventions." *Child Development* 82 (1): 405–32. https://casel.org/wp-content/uploads/2016/06/meta-analysis-child-development-1.pdf.

Dutz, M., R. Almeida, and T. Packard. 2018. *The Jobs of Tomorrow: Technology, Productivity and Prosperity in Latin America and the Caribbean*. Directions in Development Series. Washington, DC: World Bank. http://documents.worldbank.org/curated/en/242731523253230513/pdf/125044-PUB-P159108-PUBLIC-Disclose-April-11-6-4-2018-11-49-51-FullReport.pdf.

Filgueira, F., and A. Porzecanski. 2017. "Aging, the Knowledge Economy and Human Capital Creation in Latin America from Early Childhood to Secondary Education: Old and New Challenges." Background paper, World Bank, Washington, DC.

Forde, C., M. Stuart, J. Simon, L. Oliver, D. Valizade, G. Alberti, K. Hardy, V. Trappman, C. Umney, and C. Carson. 2017. *The Social Protection of Workers in the Platform Economy*. Brussels: Office for Official Publications of the European Communities. http://www.europarl.europa.eu/RegData/etudes/STUD/2017/614184/IPOL_STU(2017)614184_EN.pdf.

Frey, C., and M. Osborne. 2013. "The Future of Employment: How Susceptible Are Jobs to Computerization?" Oxford Martin Programme on Technology and Employment Working Paper, Oxford Martin School, Oxford, UK. https://www.oxfordmartin.ox.ac.uk/downloads/academic/future-of-employment.pdf.

Goldberg, L. R. 1993. "The Structure of Phenotypic Personality Traits." *American Psychologist* 48 (1): 26–34. http://psych.colorado.edu/~carey/courses/psyc5112/readings/psnstructure_goldberg.pdf.

Goos, M., and A. Manning. 2007. "Lousy and Lovely Jobs: The Rising Polarization of Work in Britain." *Review of Economics and Statistics* 89 (1): 118–33.

Goos, M., A. Manning, and A. Salomons. 2008. "Recent Changes in the European Employment Structure: The Roles of Technology, Globalization and Institutions." Lovaina: Ku Leuven. https://core.ac.uk/download/pdf/6468550.pdf.

Greiff, S., D. Holt, and J. Funke. 2013. "Perspectives on Problem Solving in Cognitive Research and Educational Assessment: Analytical, Interactive, and Collaborative Problem Solving." *Journal of Problem Solving* 5 (2): 71–91.

Heckman, J. J. 2000. "Policies to Foster Human Capital." *Research in Economics* 54 (1): 3–56.

Heckman, J. J., and T. Kautz. 2013. "Fostering and Measuring Skills: Interventions That Improve Character and Cognition." NBER Working Paper 19656, National Bureau of Economic Research, Cambridge, MA. https://www.nber.org/papers/w19656.pdf.

Heckman, J. J., J. Stixrud, and S. Urzúa. 2006. "The Effects of Cognitive and Noncognitive Abilities on Labor Market Outcomes and Social Behavior." *Journal of Labor Economics* 24 (3): 411–82. http://jenni.uchicago.edu/papers/Heckman-Stixrud-Urzua_JOLE _v24n3_2006.pdf.

Huws, U., N. Spender, D. Syrdal, and K. Holts. 2017. *Work in the European Gig Economy: Research Results from the UK, Sweden, Germany, Austria, the Netherlands, Switzerland and Italy.* Brussels: Foundation for European Progressive Studies. https://uhra.herts.ac.uk/bitstream /handle/2299/19922/Huws_U._Spencer_N.H._Syrdal_D.S._Holt_K._2017_.pdf?sequence=2.

ILO (International Labour Organization). 2016. *Non-Standard Employment Around the World: Understanding Challenges, Shaping Prospects.* Geneva: ILO. https://www.ilo.org/wcmsp5 /groups/public/---dgreports/---dcomm/---publ/documents/publication/wcms_534326.pdf.

Keister, R., and P. Lewandowski. 2016. "A Routine Transition? Causes and Consequences of the Changing Content of Jobs in Central and Eastern Europe." IBS Policy Paper 05/2016, Institute for Structural Research, Warsaw. http://ibs.org.pl/app/uploads/2016/06 /IBS_Policy_Paper_05_2016.pdf.

Maloney, W. F., and C. Molina. 2016. "Are Automation and Trade Polarizing Developing Country Labor Markets, Too?" Policy Research Working Paper 7922, World Bank, Washington, DC. https://openknowledge.worldbank.org/handle/10986/25821.

Mann, K., and L. Püttmann. 2017. *Benign Effects of Automation: New Evidence from Patent Texts.* https://papers.ssrn.com/sol3/Delivery.cfm/SSRN_ID3233471_code2678418.pdf? abstractid=2959584&mirid=1.

Messina, J., G. Pica, and A. M. Oviedo. 2016. "The Polarization Hypothesis in Latin America: How Demand Forces Are Shaping Wage Inequality?" Work in progress, shared by authors.

Michaels, G., A. Natraj, and J. van Reenen. 2014. "Has ICT Polarized Skill Demand? Evidence from Eleven Countries over Twenty-Five Years." *Review of Economics and Statistics* 96 (1): 60–77. http://eprints.lse.ac.uk/46830/1/Michaels_Natraj_VanReenen_Has-ICT-polarized -skill-demand_2014.pdf.

Möhlmann, M., and L. Zalmanson. 2017. "Hands on the Wheel: Navigating Algorithmic Management and Uber Drivers' Autonomy." Paper presented at the International Conference on Information Systems, Seoul, December 10–13.

OECD (Organisation for Economic Co-operation and Development). 2013. *OECD Guidelines on Measuring Subjective Well-being,* Paris: OECD. http://dx.doi.org/10.1787/9789264191655-en.

OECD (Organisation for Economic Co-operation and Development). 2017. *PISA 2015 Collaborative Problem-Solving Framework.* Vol. 5. Paris: OECD. https://www.oecd.org/pisa /pisaproducts/Draft%20PISA%202015%20Collaborative%20Problem%20Solving%20 Framework%20.pdf.

Packard, T., U. Gentilini, M. Grosh, P. O'Keefe, R. Palacios, D. Robalino and I. Santos. 2019. *Protecting All: Risk Sharing for a Diverse and Diversifying World of Work.* Washington, DC: World Bank. doi: 10.1596/978-1-4648-1427-3.

Schonfeld, M. 2017. *Ten Steps to Build a Work-Readiness Assessment Tool.* Washington, DC: World Bank.

Smith, R., and S. Leberstein. 2015. *Rights on Demand: Ensuring Workplace Standards and Worker Security in the On-Demand Economy.* New York: National Employment Law Project.

Spasova, S., D. Bouget, D. Ghailani, and V. Vanhercke. 2017. *Access to Social Protection for People Working on Non-Standard Contracts and as Self-Employed in Europe: A Study of National Policies.* Brussels: European Commission. https://ec.europa.eu/social/main.jsp?la ngId=en&catId=1135&newsId=2798&furtherNews=yes.

Taylor, M. 2017. *Good Work: The Taylor Review of Modern Working Practices.* London: Department for Business, Energy & Industrial Strategy.

Valenduc, G., and P. Vendramin. 2016. "Work in the Digital Economy: Sorting the Old from the New." Working Paper 2016.3, European Trade Union Institute, Brussels. http://ftu-namur .org/fichiers/Work_in_the_digital_economy-ETUI2016-3-EN.pdf.

Wichert, L., and W. Pohlmeier. 2010. "Female Labor Force Participation and the Big Five." ZEW Discussion Paper 10-003, Centre for European Economic Research, Mannheim. https:// papers.ssrn.com/sol3/Data_Integrity_Notice.cfm?abid=1551258.

World Bank. 2019. *World Development Report 2019: The Changing Nature of Work.* Washington, DC: World Bank. https://openknowledge.worldbank.org/handle/10986/30435.

3 What Is Happening in Uruguay?

Uruguay is immersed in a process of technological change that shares some similarities with other countries, but also presents some important differences. These differences deserve special attention because they relate to the effects of technological change on the labor market.

In this chapter, a brief description of changes in Uruguay's labor market in the last two decades is presented, discussing its links with technological change. Most of the analysis in this section is based on Apella and Zunino (2017), who used the conceptual framework developed by Acemoglu and Autor (2011) to characterize workers in Uruguay and their evolution. Other studies, such as OPP (2017), have produced similar results. The discussion focuses on five aspects relevant to this analysis: (1) the presence of a scale effect that could offset the negative effects of labor substitution produced by innovations and produce a net increase in labor demand; (2) the existence of a labor polarization process and its distributional impact; (3) the presence of a task-aging process; (4) the dynamics of the human capital accumulation system, considering both formal education programs and worker training programs; and (5) the role of labor market regulations and social security institutions, as well as their adaptation to a context that has changed through technological innovation.

The most prominent aspect of the labor market in Uruguay in the 2000s is a reversal of the negative trends observed in the 1990s. Most social and labor market indicators showed a negative trend during the 1990s, up to 2002–03, when the unemployment rate reached a maximum of 17 percent. Starting in 2003 employment grew rapidly, driven especially by full-time employment, and most indicators have shown strong performance in the last 15 years.

Since 2003, the labor market has improved hand in hand with the improvement in per capita GDP (figure 3.1) against a background of significant increases in commodity prices. In this new macroeconomic scenario, the employment rate reached record levels of about 60 percent in the 2010s. Similarly, the unemployment rate recorded a significant decline during the period, reaching historically low levels in 2013. Labor market indicators improved at the same time the introduction of new automation-based production technologies accelerated. For more than twenty years, commercial bank customers have been increasingly able to perform operations using automated teller machines (ATMs) and, more

FIGURE 3.1

Gross domestic product per capita, employment, and unemployment, 1995-2017

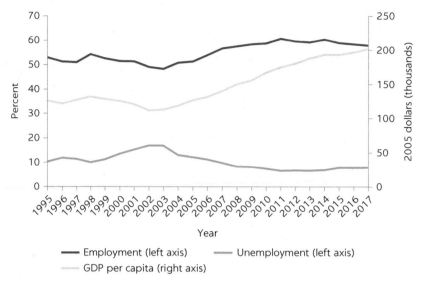

Sources: National Statistics Institute and Central Bank of Uruguay.
Note: GDP = gross domestic product.

recently, computers and mobile phones. In supermarkets, it is possible to weigh and purchase products without the assistance of employees, and e-commerce has been growing. However, despite all these potentially labor-replacing changes, unemployment and employment rates have reached their best levels in decades. This suggests, as discussed in chapter 2, that the relationship between the implementation of new automation-based production technologies and unemployment is not linear.

However, during this period there has been a change in the profile of employment. On the one hand, there has been a significant shift in employment between sectors of economic activity (figure 3.2): The most significant shift in employment has been from the industrial sector to services. In the mid-1990s, 20 percent of total employment was in industry, while in 2015 this percentage had fallen to just 11.2 percent. On the other hand, the service sector employed 32 percent of the labor force in 1990, climbing to almost 40 percent in 2015.

Apella and Zunino (2017) showed that the process of technological change did not lead to unemployment, but to a change in workers' profiles according to the tasks they perform (figure 3.3). Following the task approach proposed by Autor, Levy, and Murnane (2003) and Acemoglu and Autor (2011), among others, the authors characterized occupations according to the types of tasks developed by workers in that occupation. This perspective is relevant to assessing the impact of technological improvement on labor market structure because it helps identify the type of activity required by each occupation and assess its evolution over time. Specifically, the authors measured the intensity at which each type of task is carried out in different occupations to determine whether changes observed result, at least partially, from technological change.

Results suggest that employment profiles in Uruguay changed with respect to the intensity of the tasks performed in all occupations, shifting from manual-intensive tasks to cognitive-intensive tasks. Over the last 20 years it is

FIGURE 3.2

FIGURE 3.2

Variation in employment according to sector of activity, 1995–2015

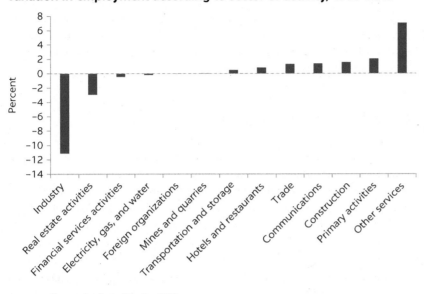

Source: Apella and Zunino 2017.

FIGURE 3.3

Change in the intensity of the tasks performed in a job, 1995–2015

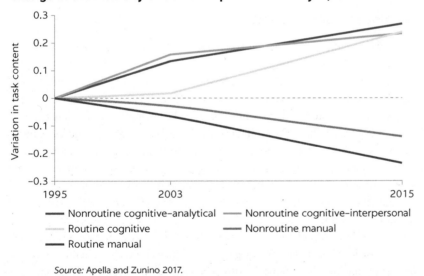

Source: Apella and Zunino 2017.

possible to observe an increase in the relative importance of nonroutine cognitive tasks, both analytical and interpersonal, with the consequent decline in medium-intensity manual tasks, both routine and nonroutine.

These trends are consistent with those observed in more developed countries. However, a discrepancy can be seen in the trend of the intensity of routine cognitive tasks, which, although declining in developed countries, grew in Uruguay. This trend implies medium-term risks, as more Uruguayans now work in occupations with a high incidence of tasks that could be replaced by automation.

If the difference observed with other countries is only temporary (that is, if the adoption of technologies that replace these tasks has been slower in Uruguay but will eventually happen), the number of workers exposed to loss of employment will be higher in the future. This type of task is mostly performed by medium-skilled, medium-wage workers; automation and displacement of these tasks will deepen distributive inequality.

SCALE EFFECT AND SUBSTITUTION EFFECT

The existence and magnitude of scale and substitution effects are difficult to measure for methodological reasons; they should be assessed across all value chains rather than at the firm or sector level, and due to the lack of public indicators on information about different sectors, their labor demand and productivity vary over time. Given this difficulty, this subsection proposes an analysis that, even if incomplete, enables an understanding some of these effects in Uruguay. Two cases are analyzed: in the financial services sector, Banco de la República Oriental del Uruguay (BROU), the biggest and oldest commercial bank in the country; and in retail, the supermarket sector. Qualitative studies were conducted using guided interviews with officials and workers in both sectors.

In both cases, the analysis focuses on the impact of introducing automated processes on the total number of workers, skill demands and necessary education of the workforce, and productivity levels.

The financial services sector

Financial services have been at the forefront of technological innovation in recent years. Banking automation is among the biggest challenges faced by the sector: Users prefer to complete financial transactions using the internet instead of visiting a local branch; the availability and popularity of mobile devices, along with easier and faster internet connections, make it simpler to complete transactions that were traditionally available only through bank offices; and basic banking transactions—such as opening bank accounts, applying for credit or debit cards, making wire transfers, and even applying for loans—can be easily and safely completed from a mobile device (EY 2016). Like most technological changes, banking automation creates both threats and opportunities. On the one hand, the demand for labor allocated to face-to-face customer care should decrease. On the other hand, the fact that users complete all their financial transactions using an electronic device generates data that maybe valuable for developing new business lines (Ghosh 2016). Consequently, there could be an increase in the demand for the labor required to process such data.

The cost reductions resulting from the ongoing technological changes also enable the emergence of new competitors in financial intermediation known as fintech, short for financial technology. Fintechs complete all transactions through the internet (such as deposits, transfers, and granting loans). These companies make the most of artificial intelligence tools and have automated not only the transactions with customers but also internal processes (Hayward and Pollari 2015). These competitors, which offer their services at a lower cost than traditional banks, boost competition in the sector. Commercial banks have a physical and contact network to their advantage but should offer services that allow them to compete with these new firms.

The current trends in the global financial sector will affect the numbers and kinds of workers, their qualifications, and the new kinds of tasks that will be needed in the banking sector. Presumably, the need for workers in all kinds of customer service jobs will decline in relative to total workers, as e-services substitute for customer-service staff. However, the growth in business scale could offset the technology substitution effect. A decline in production costs from higher labor productivity enables the offering of financial services at reduced prices, increasing the number of potential customers and transactions.

In Uruguay, the output of the financial intermediation sector, which accounted for 4 percent of GDP in 2016, grew rapidly over the 2009–16 period, showing a 75 percent increase (figure 3.4). In turn, employment in the financial sector declined during the 1990s, but rapidly recovered and, even while automation expanded in the sector, grew by 7 percent between 2009 and 2013 before leveling off. Productivity grew even faster, with apparent labor productivity increasing 63 percent from 2009 to 2016.[1]

As shown in figure 3.5, employment in the private banking sector suffered a decrease of nearly 10 percent over this period and remained steady in the public sector. The number of workers in other types of nonbanking institutions recorded an increase of 26 percent between 2009 and 2016, which more than offset the decline in the banking sector. Consequently, nonbanking institutions became the main employers within the sector. The increase in the production of financial intermediation services was strongly linked to productivity increases in the sector without significant variations in the employment level, indicating that most gains have been the result of technological innovation.

Data from the Continuous Household Survey (CHS) allow for a longer observation period at a lower level of detail. Starting in the early 2000s, the education of the sector's workers increased on average. The share of the sector's employment of persons who have completed university degrees grew significantly,

FIGURE3.4

Production, employment, and productivity in the financial sector, 2009–16

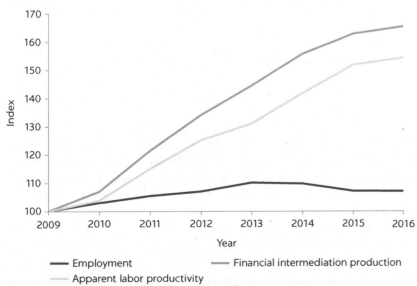

Source: Aboal et al. 2019, based on information from the Central Bank of Uruguay and the Banking Retirement and Pension Fund.

FIGURE 3.5

Employment in the financial sector, 2009–16

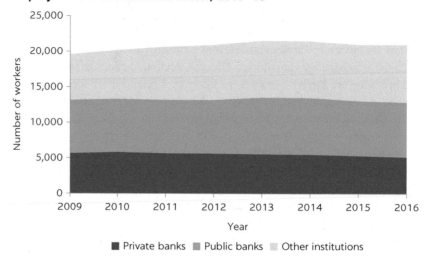

Source: Aboal et al. 2019, based on information provided by the Banking Retirement and Pension Fund.
Note: Calculations assume no changes in age-specific rates.

FIGURE 3.6

Employees in the financial services sector by qualification level, 2001–16

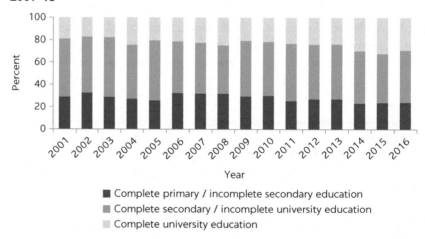

Source: Aboal et al. 2019, based on the CHS.

increasing from 19 percent to 29 percent, while workers with low and medium levels of education declined by 4 percentage points (figure 3.6). This seems to suggest that workers with higher education levels are substituting for low- and medium-qualified workers, which could be consistent with technological change in the sector.

The BROU is the largest and oldest commercial public bank operating in Uruguay. The Uruguayan commercial banking system consists of the BROU and nine private banks. In 2016, according to data from the Financial Institutions Superintendency of the Central Bank of Uruguay (table 3.1), the BROU accounted for 37 percent of loans to the nonfinancial sector and 48 percent of deposits, confirming the BROU's importance in the market.

Over the last decade, the BROU upgraded and diversified its customer service channels to respond and anticipate customers' increasing demands and as a market competition strategy. Face-to-face customer service at branch offices remains at basic levels, but there has been a dramatic increase in customer care through five digital channels: eBROU and AppBROU (e-banking); telephone banking; RedBROU (ATMs); and correspondent financial institutions (payment and collection networks through third parties, such as Abitab and Redpagos.

Figure 3.7 presents the evolution of the incorporation of these technologies. Since 2008, e-banking has been growing at a steady pace. Between 2008 and 2016, the BROU more than doubled its issuance of debit and credit RedBROU cards, and the number of eBROU customers increased tenfold.

The bank has also expanded its self-service terminals. The number of ATMs, especially mini ATMs, has increased. The mini ATMs have been available since 2014 in a correspondent network kept by the BROU through two companies engaged in payment and collections: Abitab and Redpagos. Through this mechanism, the number of ATMs has increased from 414 in 2008 to 5,217 in 2016, an increase of 1,160 percent.

TABLE 3.1 **Banking market structure, 2012–16**

Percent

	2012	2013	2014	2015	2016
Loans (% of GDP)	23	23	26	26	27
Market share					
BROU	40	38	39	38	37
Private banks	60	62	61	62	63
Deposits (% of GDP)	48	46	51	54	56
Market share					
BROU	47	47	47	45	48
Private banks	53	53	53	55	52

Source: Aboal et al. 2019, based on data from the Central Bank of Uruguay.

FIGURE 3.7

Implementation of new services by the BROU, 2008–16

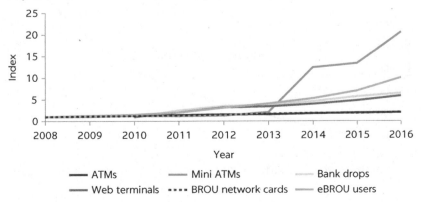

Source: Aboal et al. 2019, based on BROU Annual Reports.
Note: ATM = automated teller machine.

In 2010, the BROU launched AppBROU, an application to access eBROU from mobile devices. From eBROU or AppBROU, customers can complete transactions that were traditionally available only at a local branch. Figure 3.8 presents the increase in the number of eBROU and AppBROU customers. The upward trend between 2010 and 2014 accelerates in 2015. This change, although facilitated by technology, resulted from regulations.[2] Nevertheless, meeting customers' increasing demand for services became possible thanks to the technological changes that the BROU had undertaken years before.

The implementation of these product and process innovations has not affected the BROU's employment demand. According to guided interviews conducted with different BROU employees, the exponential increase in transactions and customers was a result of productivity increases that had no impact on employment levels. Indeed, the number of employees has remained constant—4,033 officers in 2008 versus 4,030 in 2016—because of agreements between the BROU and its unions to avoid sharp declines in employment levels.

There has, however, been an important shift in the tasks carried out by workers, from routine tasks to others that require more advanced cognitive abilities and technological skills. This trend will continue, and it is estimated that some positions will disappear as others are created, for which adaptability to change and the nuances of human relations are crucial values.

The implemented changes brought about the need to supplement and upgrade officers' training in all the products and services of the segments they manage. Likewise, the BROU sought to eliminate duplicate work and increase efficiency without disregarding each area's characteristics.

The BROU's case, though not conclusive as to the status of the financial services market, is a good example of the incorporation of new automation-based technologies. The BROU not only holds most of the market share in credit facilities and deposits, but also exerts considerable effort to incorporate digital operations technology, leading to significant productivity increases without affecting

FIGURE 3.8

eBROU and AppBROU customers, 2010–17

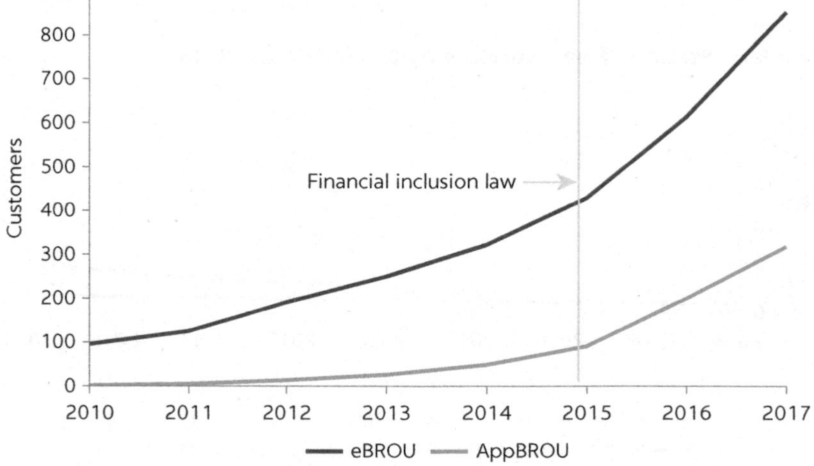

Source: Aboal et al. 2019, based on BROU Annual Reports.
Note: The Financial Inclusion Law was enacted in 2014.

the demand for employment. It has not been possible, however, to show the existence of a scale or substitution effect resulting from incorporating new production technologies in the BROU. Employment levels have not declined because of institutional agreements between the institution and unions. Workers will need to requalify for the market's new productive scenario. Not only has the qualification level of the workforce in the financial sector changed, increasing the demand for workers with a university education, but within the BROU there has been a demand for new skills to perform nonroutine cognitive tasks to supplement new intermediation digital instruments.

The retail sector

Transaction and process automation affect the nature of the retail business and lead to significant changes both in customer relations and firms' internal processes. As in the financial sector, while process automation will entail labor substitution, transaction automation is likely to involve a higher business scale. Both forces would bring about a significant change in the composition of labor demand (Deloitte 2018).

Most workers in the retail sector, including in supermarkets, perform routine manual tasks, for which only basic cognitive skills are needed. These tasks may be rendered obsolete by technological advances. Cashiers are at risk—consumers can already pay for their purchases at a terminal with little staff assistance. Furthermore, a large number of supermarket employees are stock replenishers. In the near future, with the help of sensors and robots, the number of replenishers at supermarkets could also decrease dramatically.[3]

As with financial intermediation, the automation of retail operations enables the recording of data related to consumers and their preferences. Retail stores could use this information for improved preference-based consumer identification, leading to an increase in the demand for labor in some retail areas. Workers specializing in service offerings will be needed to improve customer understanding. To process information about customers and their preferences, qualified staff could be required to manage and analyze large databases to fulfill the growing demand for forecasting (Manyika et al. 2017).

Reinforcing these processes, a large proportion of the population has access to mobile technology to get information and make purchases through the internet. In fact, an increasing portion of Uruguay's population prefers online shopping to visiting a store. E-commerce provides a better understanding of customers' consumption patterns, but also represents a direct opportunity to increase business scaling by reducing barriers to new entrants and reaching sectors of the population that stores find it difficult to serve.

General automation of the process of buying and selling goods opens the door to new participants that can compete against more traditional companies in the sector. Certainly, the currently available technology does not enable us to imagine that large retail areas will disappear in the short run. However, there *could* be a wave of new business forms that need a smaller workforce. There are new business models in sectors such as furniture or book sales. Bughin et al. (2018) identify, in the United States and some countries in Western Europe,[4] a 5 percent rate of growth in total employment in the retail sector over the 2005–16 period.

In Uruguay, production in the retail sector grew by 56 percent over the decade from 2007 to 2017 (figure 3.9). Employment remained stable over the same period, with productivity and production in the sector moving in parallel.

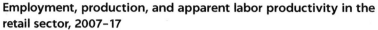

FIGURE 3.9

Employment, production, and apparent labor productivity in the retail sector, 2007–17

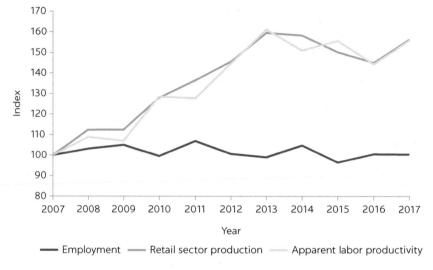

Source: Aboal et al. 2019, based on data from the Central Bank of Uruguay and the CHS.

FIGURE 3.10

Task variation intensity in the retail sector, 2003–16

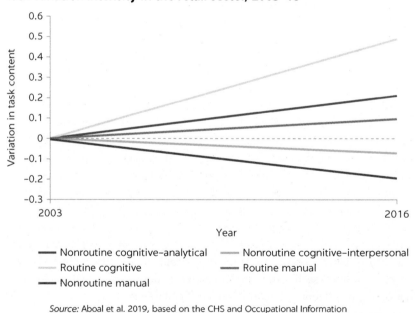

Source: Aboal et al. 2019, based on the CHS and Occupational Information Network (O*NET).

However, the task content of some jobs in the retail sector changed. Figure 3.10 shows the task variation intensity in the retail sector between 2003 and 2016. The importance of routine cognitive tasks increased significantly in this period, followed by nonroutine cognitive–analytical tasks, and a smaller increase in routine manual tasks. Conversely, there has been a reduction in nonroutine manual tasks and, to a lesser extent, in nonroutine cognitive–interpersonal tasks. The rapid increase in routine cognitive tasks could be the result of a scale factor, as the sector rapidly expanded in this period.

Several supermarkets introduced self-checkout systems, including weigh scales. The main objectives stated by industry representatives were to reduce costs, increase labor productivity, and improve security and transparency. The investments made in implementing this technological change included acquiring machinery and equipment, hardware and software, and licenses. Self-checkout arose out of the 2014 Financial Inclusion Law, which promoted a rapid expansion in the number of Uruguayans with access to electronic payment methods. Estimates suggest that, in 2015, 25 percent of payments were made through credit card and other noncash methods in supermarkets. In 2018, this percentage had risen to 70 percent. This shift in consumer behavior encouraged the introduction of self-checkout systems. As of late 2018, self-checkouts constituted 20 percent of total checkouts in retail outlets.

Self-checkout machines have not been in place long enough to assess their impact on the demand for employment. However, industry representatives expect a significant reduction in labor demand for manual and routine cognitive tasks, and an increase in demand for professionals specialized in managing the new technologies, analyzing data, and forecasting buying patterns.

LABOR FORCE POLARIZATION AND DISTRIBUTIONAL IMPACT

The subsection titled "Scale Effects and Substitution" concluded that there is no empirical evidence showing that technological change has reduced labor demand in Uruguay, whether at the aggregate level or in the two sectors examined. However, the analysis shows that there have been composition changes, with higher demand for certain types of tasks and lower demand for others. This book next explores whether these changes are part of what the literature, discussed in the subsection titled "Impact of Automation on Employment: Polarization" in chapter 2, describes as labor force polarization and their distributional impact, if any.

An empirical measurement of polarization involves ranking occupations based on income or qualification level. This work analyzes the labor polarization hypothesis using two complementary empirical approaches that rest on different strategies to rank occupations according to the qualification level required: The first strategy uses mean wages to measure polarization, while the second uses the prevalence of different types of tasks in different jobs.

For the first strategy, because the correlation between wages and years of schooling (a proxy for skill level) is not only significant and positive, but also ordinally stable, the literature has used mean wage as a variable to rank occupations in analyzing the changes in occupational structure (Autor and Dorn 2009; Goos, Manning, and Salomons 2008). Furthermore, it is assumed that hourly wage represents a good approximation of occupation average productivity, which is also positively related to the worker's skill level.

Based on this proposed definition and methodology, we ranked occupations by their average hourly wage at the beginning of the analyzed period and grouped them into 40 intervals (40-tiles).[5] We then calculated the change in the employment share of each occupational 40-tile from 2003 to 2017. The polarization hypothesis would be consistent with simultaneous growth in the relative share of occupations with higher- and lower-level productivity (hourly wages) in the labor market, as the relative share of mid-level productivity occupations decreases.

The second approach is to analyze the potential incidence of a nonneutral technical change process developed by Bussolo, Torre, and Winkler (2018). This analysis builds on the conceptual framework proposed by Acemoglu and Autor (2011). The authors classify occupations into three categories: occupations relatively intensive in routine tasks; occupations relatively intensive in nonroutine, cognitive tasks; and occupations relatively intensive in nonroutine, manual tasks.[6]

The main source of information for this report is the CHS, complemented with the O*NET database (see box 3.1), which provides information on the task content of occupations.

Figure 3.11 shows that occupations that had a relatively high hourly wage in 2003 had a larger increase in employment share in 2003–17. In addition to the increasing share of high-level productivity occupations, figure 3.11 also shows that the ratio between the change in employment share and the initial productivity level (as reflected in hourly wage) is not linear but has a J-shaped curve. In other words, the employment share in occupations with initial lower productivity is mostly stable (with a variation close to zero), declines for occupations in the mid-to-low productivity segment, and increases for those with medium and high productivity.

BOX 3.1

Occupational Information Network (O*NET) dataset

The source of information used in this study is the database developed by O*NET, which provides information on the content of occupational tasks. Since 2003, O*NET has been compiled in the United States for approximately 1,000 occupations based on the Standard Occupational Classification (SOC) and updated periodically through 2019.[a] This dataset is the successor to the Dictionary of Occupations (DOT), which is no longer updated. O*NET was started in 1998 using the Occupational Employment Statistics (OES) base of codes. Because the O*NET source was changed to SOC in 2003, the consistent measures of task content are calculated from that year. We measure the task content of each occupation using the methodology proposed by Acemoglu and Autor (2011), who use four sets of O*NET data: skills, work activities, work context, and capacities. Each contains descriptors that measure, using a scale of importance, the level, or extent, of the activity. For this report, the O*NET data from 2003 and 2018 are used to classify occupations by task performed.

To estimate the task content of each occupation in Uruguay, the elements of the tasks provided by O*NET are mapped to the classification of occupations from the CHS. In general, each country has its own version of the International Standard Classification of Occupations (ISCO); when a national classification is used, an equivalent to ISCO is applied. The classifications used in the different household surveys are codes CIUO 2008, CIUO 88, and Cota70.

In this study we assume that the characteristics that describe each occupation in Uruguay are similar to those prevailing in the United States. Because this may not be the case, the results have some bias. However, O*NET is the only available source of this type of information. The Ministry of Labor and Social Security of Uruguay has started to design and implement a similar survey at the local level, an initiative that will make both analytical work and the design and definition of training programs more relevant.

a. O*NET 24.1 (database), O*NET OnLine (accessed November 2018), www.onetonline.org.

FIGURE 3.11

Change in employment share by occupational hourly wage (40-tiles, smoothed), 2003–17

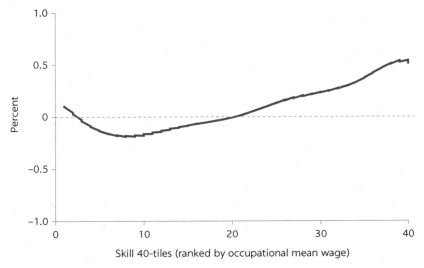

Source: Apella, Rodriguez, and Zunino 2019, based on the CHS.

FIGURE 3.12

Change in employment share by occupational category, 2003–17

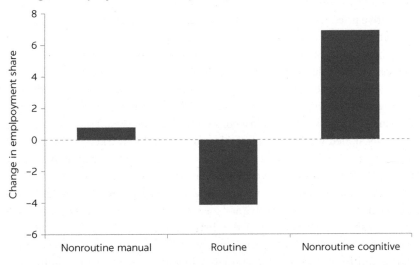

Source: Apella, Rodriguez, and Zunino 2019, based on the CHS and O*NET.

The second strategy presents evidence that confirms the incipient process of occupational polarization in the Uruguayan labor market. Nonroutine, cognitive-intensive task occupations,[7] which are linked to high qualifications and wage levels, show strong growth in their relative share of the labor market in 2003–17 (figure 3.12). At the same time, routine task-intensive occupations[8] linked to mid-qualifications and wage levels show a reduced labor market share, and nonroutine, manual task-intensive occupations,[9] characterized by lower qualifications and wage levels, exhibit a slight increase in their total employment share.

These findings are consistent with those obtained using labor income as a proxy for productivity. In both cases, labor demand seems to have remained stable for low-productivity workers, declined for those in the middle of the distribution, and increased for occupations with high productivity levels or higher qualification requirements. This shift in the labor market could pose difficulties for people who have attained a middle-school education and, therefore, bring about distributional consequences.

However, as is true for the results obtained with the first methodological approach, the variations observed in relative share by occupation are not large. Although the trends in the labor market share in Uruguay overlap significantly with the findings in developed economies, the size of the variations shows that declaring a labor polarization phenomenon is premature. The evidence gathered might suggest, however, the existence of an incipient labor polarization process that could materialize in the future. This is consistent with the nonneutral technical change hypothesis and could be the first sign of an occupational polarization process similar to that found in developed countries.

The changes in labor demand observed in Uruguay—along with changes in employment profiles, tasks performed by workers, and skills required—are associated with the growing importance of nonroutine cognitive tasks in jobs throughout the economy. This shift in tasks and required skills has been slower in Uruguay and other countries in the region than in more developed economies (Apella and Zunino forthcoming),[10] and routine cognitive tasks continue to be an important part of the day-to-day activities of most workers. Following Apella and Zunino (forthcoming), this slower adaptation process might be explained by a "relative price" effect: the cost of acquiring new production technologies may be higher than the cost borne by firms for hiring a worker.

If labor polarization has begun, as suggested by the data, the question is whether it is affecting income distribution. Demand for occupations in the mid-to-low range of productivity has declined, and demand for occupations in the high productivity range has increased. Theory indicates that this change in demand—coupled with a shift in labor supply that would result in a slow increase in highly skilled workers and in mid- and low-skilled workers competing for low-productivity jobs—could result in an increase in labor income inequality because high-range salaries would grow faster.

Descriptive evidence in Uruguay shows that, between 2003 and 2017, the growth in real wages was positive and inequality contracted sharply. Figures 3.13 and 3.14 show the evolution of the distribution of wages and monthly pay between 2003 and 2017. Between 2003 and 2017, the Gini index for wage distribution fell from 0.48 to 0.40, and labor income distribution (including the self-employed and employers) fell from 0.44 to 0.36.

With respect to the wage evolution for occupations characterized according to their task content, table 3.2 shows that, on average, higher manual task intensities—both routine and nonroutine—receive lower pay than higher routine cognitive task intensities. However, these differences have narrowed since 2003, which would reflect a relative wage improvement in less-qualified occupations, consistent with the polarization hypothesis. Occupations classified as nonroutine cognitive–analytical, however, show a higher positive difference, and this difference relative to the reference category (routine cognitive) increased in 2017 compared to 2003. Occupations classified as nonroutine cognitive–interpersonal shifted from having a lower average wage than the reference category in 2003 to having a higher average wage in 2017. These changes are very small

FIGURE 3.13

Wage distribution, 2003 and 2017

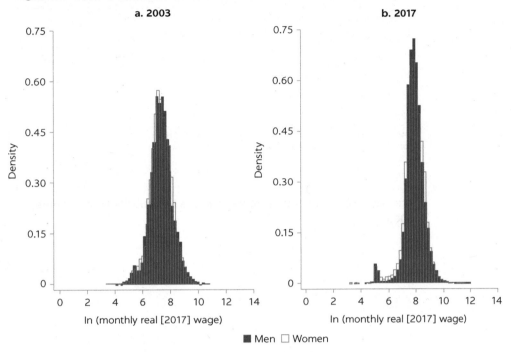

Source: Apella, Rodriguez, and Zunino 2019, based on the CHS.
Note: Wages from primary occupation deflated using consumer price index.

FIGURE 3.14

Labor income distribution, 2003 and 2017

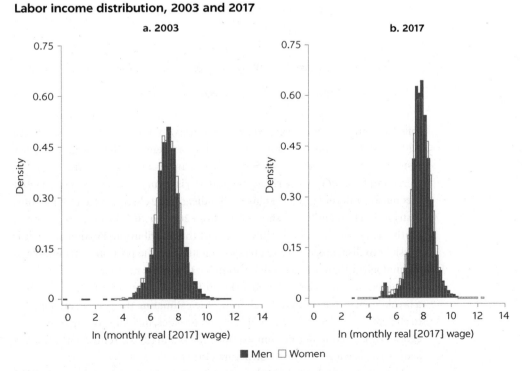

Source: Apella, Rodriguez, and Zunino 2019, based on the CHS.
Note: Unpaid family workers excluded. Wages from primary occupation deflated using consumer price index.

TABLE 3.2 **Average wage per occupational category as a proportion of wage in routine cognitive-intensive task occupations, 2003 and 2017**

TYPE OF TASK	2003	2017
Routine cognitive	1.00	1.00
Routine manual	0.65	0.70
Nonroutine cognitive–analytical	1.56	1.71
Nonroutine cognitive–interpersonal	0.91	1.10
Nonroutine manual	0.71	0.85

Source: Apella, Rodriguez, and Zunino 2019, based on the CHS and O*NET.
Note: Occupations are classified according to their task-content intensities.

FIGURE 3.15

Aggregate decomposition of the change in monthly labor income, 2003–17

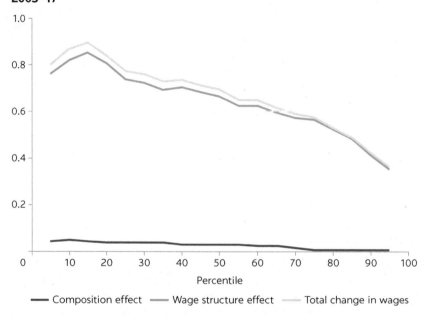

Source: Apella, Rodriguez, and Zunino 2019, based on the CHS and O*NET.

(and the statistical significance is low in all cases), but they seem to be consistent with the trends in polarization, as wages at the extremes of the distribution grew faster than the routine cognitive-intensive occupations in the middle.

A complementary, more rigorous approach is to measure the changes in labor income for different groups. Figure 3.15 indicates the changes across the income distribution percentile and shows that, from 2003 to 2017, income grew consistently faster for those in the lower part of the distribution. Furthermore, it is possible to disaggregate these changes, identifying the portions attributable to technological change and those attributable to returns to labor.

This empirical analysis—based on Firpo, Fortin, and Lemieux (2011)[11]—enables a breakdown of the changes in labor income estimating the portion attributable to changes in (1) workers' observable characteristics, including occupational categories by task content (the composition effect) and (2) the return of these characteristics on wages (the wage structure effect).

The results of this analysis show that increases in real wages between 2003 and 2017 were stronger in the lower part of the distribution and weaker in the higher part, resulting in a reduction of wage inequality. Most of this change is accounted for by the effect on returns, that is, individual wages. The composition effect (which reflects the impact of technological change) appears to be very weak; that is, the changes in workers' characteristics account only for a small part of the change in wages, and this contribution occurs homogeneously throughout the distribution.

In conclusion, Uruguay's labor market might be experiencing the early stages of a polarization process that might accelerate if technological changes that replace routine cognitive tasks are introduced at a faster pace in the future. Distributional impacts appear to have been limited so far. Jobs with a higher incidence of tasks that require mid-level skills seem to have lost returns in comparative terms, but this effect is very weak and not enough to offset the impact of other changes that, since 2003, explain an important improvement in income distribution (Amarante, Arim, and Yapor 2016). In addition to rapid economic growth from 2003 to 2017, for example, wages in Uruguay were affected by significant institutional changes, such as increases in the minimum wage, the establishment of wage councils, and the introduction of reforms in the tax and health systems.[12]

AGING OF TASKS

As discussed in chapter 2 of this book, understanding the demographic profile of those working in occupations more exposed to automation is critical to designing effective public policies. Technological change may result in a total or partial substitution for human work, and while this may have a positive impact on aggregate productivity and output, it also creates challenges for public policies designed to protect workers and facilitate their transition to more productive jobs. Policies should differ depending on the demographic profile of affected workers; in some cases it will be critical to provide basic skills to those entering the labor force, in others the focus should be on retraining more mature workers, and in others on ensuring a smooth transition to retirement.

Assessing whether there is a specific demographic profile among those in jobs more exposed to automation is difficult, due to definition issues (we can identify what tasks may be replaced, but jobs include an ever-changing combination of tasks which may be adaptable to new conditions) and lack of adequate data. However, we may consider some proxy variables, such as age profile by productivity or the task content of occupations.

The average age of workers in lower-productivity occupations has increased in the last 15 years, while the age of those in higher-productivity occupations has declined, as shown in figure 3.16. This would confirm the existence of a task-aging process, provided that the occupation's mean wage is a good proxy for productivity. Younger workers have become more concentrated in higher-productivity jobs, while older workers have moved in the opposite direction.

This trend is not fully consistent with incipient polarization. If older, less flexible workers who are in mid-productivity jobs are less able to move into higher-productivity jobs than are younger workers, and lower-productivity positions are also taken by young workers entering the labor force without adequate skills, one should expect that the mean age would increase for the mid-productivity jobs and decline for the others. However, figure 3.16 shows that the trend at the lower end of the productivity distribution is the opposite of

FIGURE 3.16

Variation in the occupational average age by hourly wage (40-tiles, smoothed), 2003–17

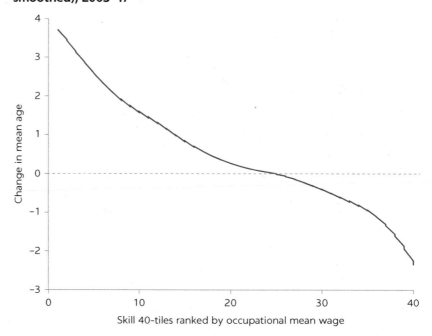

Source: Apella, Rodriguez, and Zunino 2019, based on the CHS.
Note: Skill 40-tiles are ranked by occupational mean wage.

FIGURE 3.17

Variation in the occupational average age of occupations by task-content categories

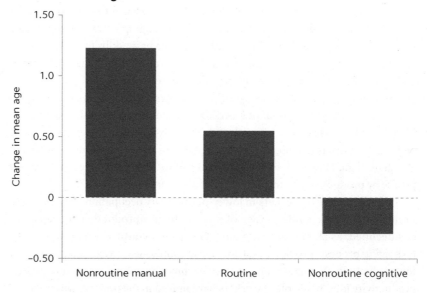

Source: Apella, Rodriguez, and Zunino 2019, based on the CHS and O*NET.

what would be expected. Older, mid-productivity workers may gradually be losing positions in the labor income distribution.

The same pattern can be observed if the task content of occupations is used as a proxy for productivity (figure 3.17). The average age of those working in nonroutine cognitive-intensive task declined by more than 0.25 year between 2003 and 2017, while those working in routine task-intensive occupations are now more than 0.5 year older than they were 15 years ago.

These observations are consistent with the hypothesis proposed by Autor and Dorn (2009) about routine tasks "growing old," as the average age of those performing them increases. However, nonroutine manual task-intensive occupations experienced the fastest rate of aging in Uruguay (more than one year between 2003 and 2017), which is inconsistent with that hypothesis. There are two possible explanations for this paradox. First, younger workers might be avoiding these occupations, given their lower salaries. Alternatively, older workers may be seeking out these occupations as a refuge against technological change and the consequent need to update their skills.

FORMAL EDUCATION AND SKILLS IN URUGUAY

Uruguay was a pioneer in 1877 in providing mandatory, free, and universal basic education. For several decades, outcomes were among the best in the region for population literacy, school attainment, and teacher quality, producing a stock of human capital that supported swift development compared with other countries in the region. However, the system gradually suffered performance problems, and the pace of improvement slowed, with its regional leadership position declining in recent decades. Although some indicators are still strong, since the turn of the 21st century, Uruguay has been ranked 78 out of 157 countries in the world (and 7 out of 10 in South America) for years of schooling by age 18 (World Bank 2018). The weaker results (and, consequently, the lack of necessary skills required in the labor market by many young workers) can be linked to issues in the sector's institutional design, which has a high degree of fragmentation; the relevance of curricular and teaching methodologies; and teacher training.

The formal education system is organized into four levels, each managed by a separate board, and the universities. Preschools (for children between 3 and 5 years of age, and mandatory at age 4) and primary schools (six years) are governed by the Initial and Primary School Board (CEIP); middle-school education (which includes a three-year basic cycle, after which students may choose between a diversified high-school degree or a technological high-school degree, is governed by the Secondary Education Board (CES) and the Technical-Professional Education Board (CETP), which also controls part of the tertiary, nonuniversity system. A fourth board controls the teacher training institutes and universities. Universidad de la República and the Technological University are autonomous. The four boards are part of an independent public entity, the National Administration of Public Education (ANEP), which in turn is directed by a national board. All boards have representatives from teachers and the government. In addition, Plan Ceibal was created in 2007 to implement the One Laptop per Child model. Since its creation, it has evolved into an agency independent of ANEP that promotes classroom innovation and provides technological solutions to schools in coordination with the respective boards. All these institutions are independent from the Ministry of Education and Culture, which has no authority over them. This complex institutional structure has resulted in an education system with limited coordination across levels and serious performance issues (INEEd 2017a; Santiago et al. 2016). The system is also highly centralized, with little opportunity for decision-making at the school level, almost no coordination on curricula or teaching strategies, and a weak accountability system.

The education system in Uruguay consists of curricula and content that fail to motivate students or teachers in the digital age, are weak in relevance, and do not address the realities of the labor markets youth will face. This combination is far from the ideal environment for developing skills for the 21st century. A shift from encyclopedic content to innovative teaching strategies, from low motivation to incentives for curiosity and experimentation, and from repetition to effective learning, would create a solid base for children and youth to develop proper skills to adapt to technological change.

Furthermore, the teaching profession fails to attract the most competent candidates, and a teaching career is often not the first choice of career for new teachers (INEEd 2017b; ANEP and CFE 2015). Although teacher salaries have doubled in the last 15 years, many teachers still do not have a formal degree (including, for example, only 38 percent of mathematics teachers). A teacher census in 2015 showed an average gap of almost five years between completing high school and starting teacher training programs, indicating that this is not the preferred career option for most teachers (ANEP and CFE 2015, 15).

The difficulties faced by Uruguay in providing children and youth with the skills required for a successful work career start in the early stages of education. The challenges of its formal system are shown by the low results that students achieve in standardized tests and in indicators such as repetition rates and school dropout rates, particularly in secondary education, and the consequent low rate of secondary school graduation, which is the last compulsory level. More than 50 percent of primary school students rank in the lowest level on standardized tests in math and reading (INEEd 2017a, 2018a), and 39 percent and 52 percent of the 15-year-old students that took the PISA tests in 2015 failed in reading and math, respectively (INEEd 2017a). The failure to develop cognitive abilities affects repetition, lag, and graduation rates. Some of these indicators have improved in recent years but are still high compared with countries at similar levels of development (ANEP and DIEE 2017).

The current education lag in Uruguay is an almost perfect predictor of school dropout rates. A longitudinal study (Cardozo 2016) revealed that, of students who took the PISA exam in 2009, only 6 percent of those with one or more years of education lag finished their secondary education by 2015, while 69 percent of those without a lag completed it (Cardozo 2016).

Not only are average results low, but inequality is high. Gaps in results between socioeconomic groups on some standardized tests are almost 50 percentage points or more (INEEd 2017a, 2018a; ANEP and DIEE 2017), and other indicators such as repetition, lag, dropout, and graduation rates also show very large gaps. One of the most relevant indicators is the rate of graduation from mandatory education: at 22 years of age only 15 percent of the population in the bottom quintile has completed all cycles, while the percentage for those in the top quintile is 71 percent (INEEd 2017a, 2017b).

The most recent studies reveal other forms of inequality, such as those related to region and gender. Except for ages 4 and 5, Montevideo has better coverage than the rest of the country. Coverage by gender is balanced for young children but is biased in favor of older girls; between the ages of 15 and 17, 86.2 percent of adolescent girls and 81 percent of adolescent boys are in the education system (INEEd 2018b).

Measurement and systematic research on socioemotional skills (SES) has only recently started in the Uruguayan educational system. Aristas, the national standardized test, recently launched by the National Institute for Education Evaluation (INEEd), has incorporated SES as one of the dimensions to be evaluated among children in grade 6 at the primary level.

The first evaluations of SES in Uruguay were obtained through the PISA assessments, which provide evidence of the relationship between socioemotional development and cognitive learning. In PISA 2012, the skills indicators with the greatest impact on the results of Uruguayan students were anxiety and self-concept. Four out of 10 students reported feeling nervous and confused during math tests, and 7 out of 10 expressed concern about the difficulties they experienced in math classes and the prospect of getting low grades (INEEd 2015, 25). It was also revealing (and worrying) that between the 2003 and 2012 assessments, Uruguayan students' evaluations of self-efficacy decreased, while the same indicator evolved positively in the rest of the world (INEEd 2015, 24).

Since the implementation of Aristas, the study of SES has been institutionalized and strengthened, and a complete conceptual framework of SES for year 6 of primary school has been developed (INEEd 2018c). The framework defines SES as "a series of cognitive, emotional and social tools whose function is to adapt the individual to the environment, and which facilitate personal development, social relationships, learning and well-being" (INEEd 2018a, 18). SES are considered a result of the personal development process, and they are learned over an individual's entire life. The skills evaluated by Aristas are shown in figure 3.18.

The evaluation of grade 6 of primary school found a wide range of development of SES (INEEd 2018a). The most salient challenges were:

- Motivation and self-regulation: low probability of using monitoring strategies (such as reviewing the task or asking questions) and low probability of motivating oneself for more challenging tasks
- Interpersonal skills: low probability of sharing feelings with friends
- Intrapersonal skills: difficulties in avoiding distraction in class or in self-control of impulses

In all the socioemotional dimensions studied, boys achieved lower averages than girls; over-age students of both sexes also achieved lower averages. Finally, students who had missed classes or who had arrived late to school in the two weeks prior to the test also achieved lower averages. These relatively poor learning and performance outcomes reveal basic and higher-order cognitive skills difficulties that start early in the children's educational trajectories. Learning is a cumulative process, and focusing on the development of skills in early stages

FIGURE 3.18

Socioemotional skills evaluated by Aristas

Motivation and self-regulation	Interpersonal skills	Intrapersonal skills
• Metacognitive self-regulation • Academic self-efficacy • Growth mind-set • Self-assessment of the task • Intrinsic motivation • Academic perseverance	• Empathy • Interpersonal skills	• Emotional regulation • Self-control

Source: INEEd 2018a.

in life is crucial: A foundation of strong skills is the first step toward providing the set of higher-order cognitive and socioemotional skills that predict adaptability to rapid changes in the work environment (World Bank 2018). Poor-quality preprimary education leaves many children unprepared to fully benefit from primary and higher levels of school. The serious performance issues of the education system can be seen through the cumulative skills gaps shown by the evidence obtained through tests, and by the low efficiency indicators that start as early as the first years of the primary level.

Although the traditional education structures are struggling to perform effectively, there are several programs jointly implemented by the education authorities and Plan Ceibal. Some are pilots, whose scaling-up could be a challenge, while others are already fully developed. The most noteworthy are (1) Computational Thinking, (2) Ceibal in English, (3) Youth Programming, (4) Global Learning Network, and (5) the Data Science Diploma. These initiatives break the traditional curricular structure, using project-based approaches, remote teaching, and programs that span grades and education levels to promote the development of critical skills (box 3.2).

BOX 3.2

Innovative programs in Uruguay's education system

Despite the challenges, Uruguay is implementing initiatives that promote a skills-oriented education, project-based learning, and problem-solving strategies that cut across traditional school subjects. Bringing these initiatives to a larger scale requires adapting governance structures and designing and implementing evaluation systems, to produce evidence useful for producing strategies for the acquisition of long-term skills.

Computational thinking: Computational thinking is a problem-solving methodology that has been included in the curricula of countries such as Costa Rica, Estonia, Finland, Germany, Mexico, and the United Kingdom. This approach involves learning and applying the four pillars of the computational thinking method (decomposition, pattern recognition, pattern generalization and abstraction, and algorithm design). It is not restricted to coding or programming, but involves learning logic, algorithm, and problem-solving techniques, while promoting other skills such as formulating ideas, creativity, and design. The program is implemented by the Initial and Primary School Board (CEIP) with support from Plan Ceibal and the National Administration of Public Education (ANEP) in public primary schools. Classes are offered through video-conferencing equipment that Plan Ceibal installed in schools. In 2018, it reached 476 groups of 5th and 6th grade children in 222 schools throughout the country, totaling 13 percent of the school-age population. In 2019 the plan is to reach more than 50 percent of the school-age population.

Ceibal in English: This program aims at developing cognitive and communication skills, along with English fluency for using digital technology. The program is implemented in primary schools (4th and 6th grades) and in secondary schools (1st and 3rd years). In 2018, approximately 70 percent of students in these grades participated in the program while the remaining 30 percent received traditional classes. Classes are offered remotely by a teacher who may or may not be in Uruguay, with a second teacher present in the classroom for support and classroom management. The program also trains teachers in English. In secondary schools, the program is called "conversation class," and its main goal is to improve oral ability. The class is offered once a week, remotely, by a native English speaker, together with the classroom teacher. Program evaluations show that there are no significant differences in learning between remote and on-site teaching. Thus, English teaching can be scaled-up to all schools,

continued

Box 3.2, *continued*

beyond the local availability of second-language teachers, and still preserve the quality of learning.

Youth Programming: This Plan Ceibal program, aimed at providing skills relevant for information and communication technology (ICT) jobs, was launched in 2016 to train youth who finished the basic cycle of secondary school in programming languages, English, and socioemotional skills. A women-only cohort, aimed at reducing the gender gap among information technology professionals, was opened in 2019 and attracted 700 participants. This project is a public-private initiative, supported by the Uruguay Chamber of Information Technologies (CUTI).

Global Learning Network: This program aims at promoting the development of superior cognitive and socioemotional skills among students from all socioeconomic levels. The program is designed to promote, systematize, and evaluate a system of educational practices that develop learning skills for the 21st century, using technology as a tool for access and acceleration of pedagogical results. The interventions focus on six competencies known as the "six Cs": character; citizenship; communication; critical thinking and problem-solving; collaboration; and creativity and imagination. The program is open to students from all education subsystems, as well as teachers and directors. By the end of 2018, there were 395 primary and secondary schools in the program. The program is monitored and evaluated by Plan Ceibal. The network is expanding and is now an international project that includes schools from Australia; Canada; Hong Kong SAR, China; Finland; New Zealand; the Netherlands; and the United States.

Data Science Diploma: The program aims at developing human capital specialized in digital skills, targeting youth in Uruguay. The program, which began in May 2019, consists of formal training that lasts 18 months, with remote classes and 8 weeks of intensive classes in Uruguay. The program is coordinated by Plan Ceibal, the National Agency for Research and Innovation (ANII), and the Technological University of Uruguay (UTEC), with academic support from the Massachusetts Institute of Technology (MIT) and Harvard University. Students completing the training will receive formal accreditation from UTEC, MIT, and Harvard.

LABOR MARKET INSTITUTIONS AND SOCIAL PROTECTION

As in other countries, the gig economy in Uruguay has gained attention from researchers and policy makers, as the number of firms offering platforms and the workers enrolled in them has grown. Although crowdworking does not seem to have had an impact on total employment (although there are no data on whether workers from Uruguay are participating in crowdwork projects in other parts of the world), on-demand working platforms have expanded rapidly (box 3.3). PedidosYa, a pioneering platform that offers delivery services throughout Latin America, was created in Uruguay in 2009, and its headquarters are still in Montevideo. Other platforms—such as Soy Delivery, Rappi, Glovo, and Uber Eats—have entered the market more recently, since 2015. On Transportation, Easy Taxi, and Uber launched in Uruguay in 2015, and other platforms (Uruguay Presente, Cabify) have also entered the market to compete with Uber. There are no official figures for the number of workers providing services through these platforms in Uruguay, but an estimate published by a group of workers that is organizing a union put this figure at 8,000 deliverers as of April 2018. Uber counts almost 4,800 drivers; 25 percent of them, however, are not active workers, and a similar number spends less than two hours a day on the activity (Marquez and Goday 2019).

The demographic profile of workers participating in these platforms is similar to that found in other countries and discussed in chapter 1 of this book—most workers are young and, in many cases, students. However, an important distinction between workers in more developed countries and those in Uruguay is that,

BOX 3.3

Case study: History of delivery services in Uruguay

Delivery services in Uruguay, especially those by restaurants and drugstores, expanded during the 1990s through a model known as "external waiters." This occupation was formally recognized as an employment category by authorities, and working conditions were part of the collective bargaining process. In the early 2000s, these services began to be outsourced. Delivery companies would offer the service to restaurants, and then handle staff and logistics. This change can be explained by the rapid expansion in demand for these services, which created the market, and the high transaction costs that individual firms incurred managing delivery staff directly.

As digital platforms became a reality, delivery services were one of the first activities offered through them. In the mid-2010s, PedidosYa was created in Uruguay, providing an effective tool to connect demand and supply of goods and services. The service became more visible on both sides of the market, enabling quick growth in scale and efficiency.

The original business model was a simple contact application, but as issues of service quality surfaced and deliveries became slow, Pedidos Ya adjusted its business strategy and hired deliverers as salaried workers.

Thus, PedidosYa staff are now standard formal wage earners, and their contracts comply with social security regulations as well as labor rules (such as paid vacations or minimum wages).

However, a new problem of agency between employer and employee resulted from the incentives created by this model. Employees receive payment of the minimum wage regardless of the volume of orders delivered, and because delivery jobs could be rejected over their mobile phones, employees had an incentive to work less.

At present, no solution has been proposed. Legislation allows for a proportional minimum wage, but its implementation has been complex. A supplementary strategy has also been discussed, which would align the company's and employees' interests (principal-agent) through an adjustment of dismissal proceedings, allowing, for example, the rejection of jobs as a cause for dismissal.

Pedidos Ya currently competes in the market with other apps such as Glovo and Rappi, which imitate Uber's business model. Even though the number of these digital platforms has increased, their relevance as measured by the number of workers is low, as is their impact on working conditions.

in Uruguay, these earnings are more often workers' main source of income (Erosa 2017; De Marco 2019).

Authorities in Uruguay are looking for ways to regulate the activities of these platforms (Da Silva 2019). The 2015–19 budget law contained a proposal requiring that platforms be equally responsible for taxes and fees with those offering services through them, with a focus on transportation services (such as Uber) and temporary housing (such as Airbnb). In March 2016, the government sent a draft law to Congress to regulate "Service Provision through Information Platforms." This proposal was approved by the lower chamber but was never discussed in the Senate. The proposed legislation was a short document that did not modify any regulation, but explicitly stated that activities implemented through these new platforms were subject to existing rules. In 2017, a decree was issued ordering motorcycle deliverers to complete a training course taught by the National Institute of Employment and Professional Training (INEFOP) and the Traffic Safety Unit (UNASEV).

Uber is by far the largest platform in Uruguay. Legal and judicial disputes followed its local launch at the end of 2015, as a result of the objections to its operation by taxi drivers and the city government of Montevideo. In December 2016, the city issued Decree Law 36197, authorizing "the modality of paid transportation of passengers in private vehicles hired through e-platforms," which set forth duties such as payment of a royalty to the city, maintaining cars in proper condition, and complying with tax and social security obligations. Registration of new drivers was closed in early 2018.

One way to analyze the scope of the phenomenon in Uruguay is to see whether it led to significant changes in the labor market structure and, specifically, whether the number of independent workers, as individuals registered in digital platforms are generally characterized, has increased. Faster job rotation could also be expected because of technological changes, as well as changes in the number of part-time jobs. These analytical strategies may offer some hints about trends, although the hints will be limited in scope because the employment market survey does not identify platform work as a category and the surveys cannot reliable identify relatively small changes. Data from the CHS for seven years between 1995 and 2018 were analyzed.

Figure 3.19 illustrates the distribution of workers by type of employment. No significant changes can be seen in the employment structure between 1995 and 2018; wage earners have represented approximately 70 percent of all workers during this period. The percentage of independent workers has also been stable, at about 20 percent in the 1990s and then between 20 percent and 25 percent starting in about 2000.

The average length of employment among salaried workers has been increasing in recent years, a trend that is inconsistent with the hypothesis of an acceleration of job rotation (figure 3.20). Similarly, part-time employment has been very stable for both salaried and independent workers (with a decline among independent workers in the late 1990s), again showing a trend that is not consistent with a large growth of new forms of employment (figure 3.21).

The percentage of employees working part-time (less than 30 hours per week) has also remained stable, at about 22 percent (figure 3.22). Educational attainment among independent workers has increased, but not at a rate that would indicate an increase in highly skilled workers moving from traditional to platform-based jobs (figure 3.23).

Empirical evidence at the aggregate level shows that the impact of the gig economy on Uruguay's labor market has been very small. The gig economy may, however, already be important in some sectors, and its impact may increase, requiring appropriate public policy responses.

FIGURE 3.19

Share of different forms of employment, 1995–2018

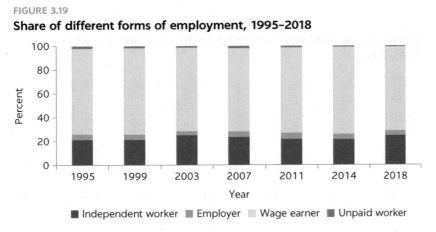

Source: World Bank calculations based on CHS.

FIGURE 3.20

Years on the job for salaried workers, 1995–2018

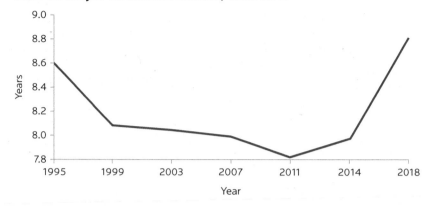

Source: World Bank calculations based on CHS.

FIGURE 3.21

Average hours worked, 1995–2018

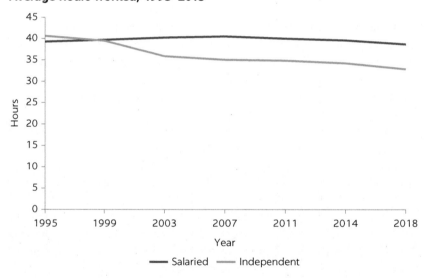

Source: World Bank calculations based on CHS.

FIGURE 3.22

Percentage of employees working less than 30 hours per week, 1995–2018

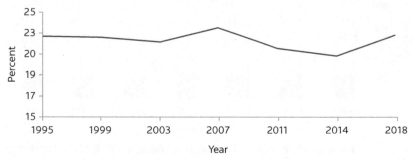

Source: World Bank calculations based on CHS.

FIGURE 3.23

Independent workers by the highest level of education achieved, 1995–2018

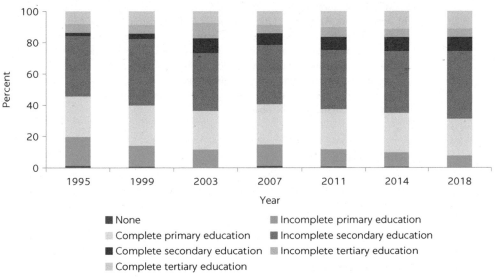

Source: World Bank calculations based on CHS.

NOTES

1. Apparent labor productivity is a traditional indicator defined as the ratio between the output generated at a given time and the number of persons employed.
2. Law No. 19,210 (the Financial Inclusion Law), enacted on May 9, 2014, and characterized as the "population's access to financial services and promotion of the use of electronic payment systems" regulates and promotes certain economic transactions. Sections 10 and 12 establish that "the payment of remunerations and any other monies to which workers are entitled . . . shall be made through crediting into an account held with a financial intermediation institution or electronic money instrument."
3. The International Federation of Robotics estimated that, in 2018, 35 million robots would be sold worldwide to be used in the services area (Ghosh 2016). In 2015, that figure amounted to only 152,400 units.
4. The study included Austria, Belgium, Denmark, Finland, France, Germany, Greece, Italy, the Netherlands, Norway, Spain, Sweden, Switzerland, and the United Kingdom.
5. Although occupations are usually grouped in hourly wage percentiles, the analysis in this work is based on 40 intervals. We use a lower number of categories because, in practice, data from the CHS for the period do not enable occupations to be monitored at the hourly wage level of disaggregation. Specifically, the CHS works with the three-digit International Standard Classification of Occupations (ISCO) code, which permits the monitoring of a total of 132 occupations.
6. Grouping occupations into three exclusive categories limits the analysis because, to a lesser or greater extent, each occupation involves different types of tasks. The grouping strategy necessarily implies identifying the most relevant tasks on a case-by-case basis. Occupations characterized one way, however, could also be characterized by a significant intensity in other types of tasks.
7. Includes occupations such as production and operations department managers, nursing and midwifery professionals, professionals such as medical doctors, biologists, agronomists, biologists, veterinarians, pharmacologists, accountants and business administration specialists, and computer programmers and computer systems analysts.
8. Includes occupations such doorkeepers, security guards and related workers, seamstresses, embroiderers and knitters, general office clerks and secretaries, typists and word-processor and related operators, and machine and tool operators.

9. Includes occupations such as mining and mineral processing plant operators, fashion and other models, treasury and social security officials, and locomotive engine drivers and switch operators.

10. According to World Bank (2016), countries such as Austria, Finland, France, Greece, the United Kingdom, and the United States, have experienced high levels of labor polarization, with a simultaneous increase in labor force participation by workers with high and low skills, and a decline of those in the middle of the distribution.

11. See appendix B for a methodological discussion.

12. In July 2007, an income tax was introduced, which had a direct impact on workers in the higher part of the wage distribution.

REFERENCES

Aboal, D., A. López, R. Maurizio, P. Queraltó, and E. Tealde. 2019. "Digitalización y empleo en Uruguay en los sectores bancario, forestal y supermercados: Impactos y estrategias para la adaptación del capital humano." Background paper, World Bank, Washington, DC.

Acemoglu, D., and D. Autor. 2011. "Skills, Tasks and Technologies: Implications for Employment and Earning." In *Handbook of Labor Economics*, vol. 4, edited by O. Ashenfelter and D. E. Card, 1043–1171. Amsterdam: Elsevier.

Amarante, V., R. Arim, and M. Yapor. 2016. "Decomposing Inequality Changes in Uruguay: The Role of Formalization in the Labor Market." *IZA Journal of Labor and Development* 5 (1): 1–20.

ANEP (National Administration of Public Education) and CFE (Education Training Council). 2015. *Los estudiantes de formación en educación: Estudio sobre datos aportados por el censo de estudiantes del CFE 2014–2015*. Montevideo: CFE.

ANEP (National Administration of Public Education) and DIEE (Research, Evaluation and Statistic Division). 2017. *Uruguay en PISA 2015*. Montevideo: National Administration of Public Education.

Apella, I., L. Rodriguez Chamussy, and G. Zunino. 2019. "Cambio Tecnológico en Uruguay: Polarización del mercado de trabajo y efectos distributivos." Background paper, World Bank, Washington, DC.

Apella, I., and G. Zunino. 2017. "Technological Change and the Labor Market in Argentina and Uruguay. A Task Content Analysis." Policy Research Working Paper 8215, World Bank, Washington, DC. https://openknowledge.worldbank.org/handle/10986/28550.

Apella, I., and G. Zunino. Forthcoming. "Technological Change and Labor Market Trends in Latin America and the Caribbean: A Task Content Approach."

Autor, D., and D. Dorn. 2009. "This Job Is Getting Old: Measuring Changes in Job Opportunities Using Occupational Age Structure." *American Economic Review: Papers & Proceedings* 99 (2): 45–51.

Autor, D., F. Levy, and R. Murnane. 2003. "The Skill Content of Recent Technological Change: An Empirical Exploration." *Quarterly Journal of Economics* 118 (4): 1279–1333. https://economics.mit.edu/files/11574.

Bughin, J., E. Hazan, S. Lund, P. Dahlstrom, A. Wiesinger, and A. Subramaniam. 2018. "Skill Shift, Automation and the Future of the Workforce." Discussion paper, McKinsey Global Institute.

Bussolo, M., I. Torre, and H. Winkler. 2018. "Accounting for the Role of Occupational Change on Earnings in Europe and Central Asia." IZA Conference Working Paper. http://conference.iza.org/conference_files/WoLabConf_2018/torre_i26373.pdf.

Cardozo, S. 2016. *Trayectorias educativas en la educación media*. Montevideo: INEEd. https://www.ineed.edu.uy/images/pdf/trayectorias-educativas.pdf.

Da Silva, M. 2019. "El País: Negocios." https://sso.elpais.com.uy/cas/login?showAs=premium&service=https%3A%2F%2Fnegocios.elpais.com.uy%2Fcas-check&utm_source=exclusive_content.

De Marco, J. 2019. "El País." https://sso.elpais.com.uy/cas/login?showAs=premium &service=https%3A%2F%2Fwww.elpais.com.uy%2Fcas-check&utm_source=exclusive _content.

Deloitte. 2018. *Global Powers of Retailing 2018: Transformative Change, Reinvigorated Commerce.* New York: Deloitte.

Erosa, D. 2017. "Correspondencia de Prensa." https://correspondenciadeprensa.com/2017 /07/21/uruguay-los-delivery-un-oficio-que-avanza-entre-la-informalidad-laboral-y-la -precariedad-salarial/.

EY (Ernst & Young LLP). 2016. *The Digital Bank: Tech Innovations Driving Change at U.S. Banks.* https://bpi.com/wp-content/uploads/2018/07/20161201_tch_ey_fintech_paper.pdf.

Firpo, S., N. M. Fortin, and T. Lemieux. 2011. "Occupational Tasks and Changes in the Wage Structure." IZA Discussion Paper 5542, Institute for the Study of Labor, Bonn. http://ftp.iza .org/dp5542.pdf.

Ghosh, B. 2016. "Intelligent Automation: The Essential New Co-Worker for the Digital Age." *Technology Information Blog,* January 27. https://www.accenture.com/us-en/blogs /blogs-industrial-automation-and-robotic-process-automation.

Hayward, B., and I. Pollari. 2015. *The Perfect Storm of Technology and Capital Markets: The Modern History of FinTech.* https://assets.kpmg/content/dam/kpmg/pdf/2015/06 /technology-capital-markets-fintech-history-article-june-2015.pdf.

INEEd (National Institute for Education Evaluation). 2015. *Habilidades no-cognitivas y desempeños en matemática entre los estudiantes uruguayos evaluados en PISA 2012.* Montevideo: INEEd. https://www.ineed.edu.uy/images/pdf/informeweb.pdf.

INEEd (National Institute for Education Evaluation). 2017a. *Informe sobre el estado de la educación 2015–2016. Síntesis y desafíos.* Montevideo: INEEd.

INEEd (National Institute for Education Evaluation). 2017b. *Informe de la Encuesta Nacional Docente 2015.* Montevideo: INEEd.

INEEd (National Institute for Education Evaluation). 2018a. *ARISTAS 2017: Informe de resultados de tercero y sexto de educación primaria.* Montevideo: INEEd.

INEEd (National Institute for Education Evaluation). 2018b. *Reporte del Mirador Educativo 1: Desigualdades en el acceso a la educación obligatoria.* Montevideo: INEEd.

INEEd (National Institute for Education Evaluation). 2018c. *Aristas: Marco general de la evaluación.* Montevideo: INEEd. https://www.ineed.edu.uy/images/Aristas/Publicaciones /Marcos/Aristas_MarcoGeneral_v07.pdf.

Manyika, J., M. Chui, M. Miremadi, J. Bughin, K. George, P. Wilmott, and M. Dewhurst. 2017. *A Future That Works: Automation, Employment and Productivity.* San Francisco: McKinsey Global Institute. http://hdl.voced.edu.au/10707/421215.

Marquez, G., and L. Goday. 2019. *Study of the Operation of Transportation Industry through Applications and Its Consequences in the Paid Passenger Transportation Sector in the City of Montevideo.* Montevideo: Intendencia Municipal de Montevideo.

OPP (Oficina de Planeamiento y Presupuesto). 2017. "Automatización y Empleo en Uruguay." *Serie de Divulgación, Volumen II.* Montevideo: OPP.

Santiago, P., B. Avalos, T. Burns, A. Morduchowicz, and T. Radinger. 2016. *OECD Reviews of School Resources: Uruguay 2016.* Paris: OECD. http://dx.doi.org/10.1787/9789264265530-en.

World Bank. 2016. *World Development Report 2016: Digital Dividends.* Washington, DC: World Bank. https://openknowledge.worldbank.org/handle/10986/23347.

World Bank. 2018. *World Development Report 2018: Learning: to Realize Education's Promise.* Washington DC: World Bank. https://openknowledge.worldbank.org/handle/10986/28340.

4 Public Policy

Technological innovations may result in sustained increases in productivity, which can improve social welfare, especially in countries, such as Uruguay, whose populations are aging. However, innovations may also result in the replacement of human workers with automation, generating risks such as technological unemployment and labor market polarization. These effects may be balanced (and possibly reversed) if an increase in the production scale at the firm, sector, or value chain level offsets the reduction in costs produced by the changes in technology. This requires workers to have the skills to adapt to new demands in the labor market, and labor regulations and social insurance institutions must adapt to provide effective protection while smoothing the transition.

The empirical evidence for these processes in Uruguay is very limited, in part because not enough data are available to assess the magnitude of some of them and in part because the available data indicate that changes in aggregate labor demand and market polarization produced by technological changes are still small. Although the available information does not indicate that technological innovations are causing serious problems for Uruguay, their effects may be more apparent as innovations continue to be introduced and disseminated throughout the economy. Discussing public policies that would respond to these trends is relevant because they might become critical to ensuring continued economic and welfare growth in coming years.

This book has addressed several aspects of the relationship between technological change and labor markets: (1) the potential net result between the scale effect (the increase in the demand for employment resulting from reduced costs and increased production levels) and the substitution effect (the crowding-out of labor by the introduction of automation in routine tasks), (2) the risk of labor market polarization and its corresponding distributional impact, (3) the demographic dynamics of tasks that tend to disappear with technological change, (4) the role of skills in technological change and the current policies in Uruguay to provide future and current workers with such skills throughout their lives, and (5) the impact that technology-driven changes in the labor market could have on labor regulation and social protection institutions.

The empirical evidence on the dynamics of these processes in Uruguay was presented in chapter 3, where we showed that

- technological change is affecting labor demand composition and wage structures, but not as clearly aggregate labor demand;
- polarization and task-aging processes appear to exist incipiently;
- the basic education and skills-generating systems have had serious performance difficulties in recent decades and are not providing the labor force with necessary skills, despite the development of certain initiatives; and
- the gig economy has been growing and is relevant in some sectors, where regulations and institutions have been under discussion, but it is still small enough not to show on aggregate labor market indicators.

Given these findings, public policy should focus on taking advantage of opportunities to increase productivity and aggregate output and manage the potential adverse effects of new production technologies on worker welfare and employment conditions. There are at least five public policy areas that should be considered in this discussion: (1) encouraging the incorporation of new production technologies in sectors where increases in efficiency and productivity result from increases in production scale, which bring about an increase in the demand for labor; (2) promoting and facilitating the acquisition of relevant skills and knowledge for future workers, based on observed changes in the occupational structure and the potential acceleration of the automation of routine tasks; (3) improvement in the skills and abilities of young workers in occupations with a high content of routine cognitive tasks; (4) adapting labor regulations and social protection systems to provide effective support to older workers exposed to a higher risk of automation; and (5) adapting labor regulations and social protection systems to facilitate the introduction of new technology while adequately protecting the population.

PROMOTING THE SCALE EFFECT

Innovations that increase productivity also tend to replace human work on some tasks. This substitution effect may result in a decline of labor demand but can be offset if the reductions in production costs generate a scale effect, facilitating increases in total output for the firms, sectors, or value chains.

Introducing new productive technologies is critical to increasing productivity and maintaining competitiveness in global trade. Public policies should promote this process, including the adoption of innovations that result in an increase in the demand for labor through scale effects. Uruguay, like other countries, has sectoral policies that promote investment and innovation. These policies are usually selected based on their potential contribution to economic growth, their impact on international trade, and their effects on local development. Their impact on labor demand through the scale effect, however, a factor that could be incorporated in the design of policy, is rarely assessed.

Technological innovations are not homogeneous in their direct impact on labor markets or in the sectors in which these innovations are applied. Understanding the market structure of different sectors is critical to designing effective policy interventions. The market structure in which firms participate affects the impact of new technology on labor demand and social welfare. The adoption of technological change is a decision made by individual firms after comparing the expected benefits of the new technology with the benefits of its traditional production function. Productive process innovations reduce average and marginal costs, and net positive scale effects may occur if the efficiency gains result in lower prices. Lower prices may in time trigger higher demand for the affected goods and services and, consequently, higher labor demand for those involved in their production.

However, the adoption of new technology also has fixed costs that, depending on the type of innovation and the magnitude of the reduction of marginal and average costs, may act either as a barrier to entry of new competitors or remove preexisting barriers. The impact of the innovations on these barriers will depend on the structure and behavior of each market; a case-by-case study is necessary to effectively design and implement sector-specific promotion policies.

Because market structures are heterogeneous, the effects of innovation processes are asymmetrical, with differences among participants in productive dynamics and the capacity to generate jobs. The adoption of new technology can transform market structures significantly. However, the direction of change in these transformations depends on preexisting market heterogeneity, especially the level of productivity.

New technology may increase or decrease heterogeneity in markets, depending on its effect on competitiveness and optimal scale. If technological progress has different effects on different firms, the benefits may, on the one hand, be accessible only to a small number of firms, and competition may decline. On the other hand, innovations that are easily adopted by all firms in a sector may promote competition. Therefore, the prerequisite for any public initiative to encourage the adoption of technological innovations should be an understanding of market structure, identifying its main participants and its degree of heterogeneity.

The discussion of optimal policy interventions can begin with extreme cases. First, where the incorporation of a new production technology creates or intensifies the barriers to entry for new competitors, increasing the market concentration of incumbent firms, which will be encouraged to increase prices and decrease production. In this case, the public policy aimed at promoting the adoption of new technology should be accompanied by regulatory policy to limit the incumbent's market power (the relationship between price and quantity). In a second example, new production technology could weaken entry barriers by reducing fixed costs, thus facilitating the entry of new participants and increasing production and employment. The creation of commercial platforms connected through the internet, where buyers and sellers gather with minimum transaction costs, is an example. This type of technology reduces fixed costs for the platform's clients and, accordingly, barriers to entry, increasing competition by favoring the participation of small and medium-sized producers. In this context, public policy should support the adoption of new technology because the efficiency gains would result in lower prices and increased demand. In a third scenario, technology results in the creation of new markets or new products. In this case, policy should support the expansion and consolidation of the market because the net result of the scale and substitution effects is always positive.

ENCOURAGING SKILLS FOR THE JOB OF THE FUTURE

Uruguay's formal education system faces serious difficulties in providing new generations with adequate skills to perform successfully in the labor market. In the past, the most serious challenge has been the coverage (student retention) of the system, as many young Uruguayans drop out of school before completing their basic education. The quality of education has also been an issue, as shown by the standardized tests results discussed in chapter 3. A third dimension will become even more critical, however, as technological changes affect the labor market, shifting the demand for skills from the traditional technical to more sophisticated, higher-order cognitive and socioemotional, a need that the traditional education model is not designed to address. Hence, policy initiatives to improve the skill provision system in Uruguay need to focus not only on coverage and quality but also on relevance, moving away from the traditional encyclopedic curriculum and toward a model that prepares students for a rapidly evolving labor market.

Investing in the development of relevant skills is necessary for macroeconomic reasons and to reduce the risk of labor force polarization. The search for quality employment would be further impaired for workers with inadequate skills, and sectors that are unable to find workers with the proper skills may be unable to take advantage of potential growth from the adoption of innovative technology (Dutz, Almeida, and Packard 2018).

Education policy could be strengthened through the introduction of changes and innovations. The most challenging areas are (1) governance of the education system as a whole, (2) curriculum revision, (3) the reinforcement of training for teachers at entry and during service, and (4) increasing management autonomy of schools.

With respect to governance, reorganizing the system with more strategic and less collective management could make it more effective, eliminating overlapping roles and inefficiencies. The governance structure should focus on the skills development process, instead of the forced artificial divisions used in the past. The educational path should start at the first childhood stage (about 3 years of age), go through adolescence, and end in the higher middle and higher education cycles.[1] Local evidence reveals that coordination between the different levels of education is essential to avoid forcing students to move through organizational divisions, especially those that currently result in the high rates of grade repetition that are seen between the preschool and primary cycles and between the primary and secondary cycles, which cause bottlenecks in students' advancement.

The integration of educational paths should also be reflected in the content of the curricula. The continuation and strengthening of emerging efforts by the National Administration of Public Education (ANEP) to develop a more integrated curriculum requires intensifying the focus on competencies that cross-cut every subject, with well-defined graduation profiles. Subjects should be reorganized around areas of knowledge, starting with elementary education, deepening the focus on the development of socioemotional skills and on active pedagogies, with room for pedagogical innovation (Kärkkäinen 2012). In addition, curricular changes and new pedagogical practices should take advantage of innovations that customize the learning process. Although 20th-century schools were devised as unified producers of knowledge, technology currently enables the use of adaptive platforms and customizable options, adjusted to each student's interests and without forcing them to learn at the same pace as others (Filgueira and Porzecanski 2017). Rigid curricular content restricts the adoption of these innovations, repressing learning opportunities that are already available for most public schools in Uruguay.

A renewed governance model for the education system in Uruguay should also offer greater management autonomy to schools to allow them to be more dynamic and to provide them with the tools to achieve better learning results. Schools would benefit from being more autonomous in the areas of human resources management and the planning and organization of teaching. This model should be accompanied by programs that enable school directors to develop the skills required for managerial and leadership positions, including the use and planning of resources, as well as the training and supervision of teachers at all levels (World Bank 2018).

Technical education, in the form of basic professional training, should be maintained and improved as an effective solution for the middle education dropout problem and to reduce the difficulties of integration into the labor market. In the medium term, however, technical education should not be considered an educational option separate from general secondary studies but, instead, should be embedded in the general curriculum. Links between the labor market and the education system should be introduced or strengthened. Education systems that have improved their results relative to other countries did so through the inclusion in their curricula of education components relevant for the labor market; the universality of higher secondary education has been rarely achieved through the application of curricula exclusively focused on education for the university (Filgueira and Porzecanski 2017). Expanding practices such as internships as part of the school curriculum could retain students interested in entering the labor market, instead of forcing them to choose between completing their education or dropping out to work.

Integration between technical and general education is consistent with current empirical evidence on employers' increasing interest in higher-order cognitive and socioemotional skills, instead of specific, too-narrow technical skills related to traditional occupations. Policy makers sometimes identify traditional work skills with technical skills, but employers do not necessarily do so. Technical skills are considered a supplement to other foundational skills, implying that shifting the emphasis from labor training to the strengthening of higher-order cognitive and socioemotional skills at young ages might be advisable. Training in specific work areas, especially at the end of higher secondary education, should be combined with cognitive and socioemotional skills related to the general education curriculum. In other words, the fragmentation of the education system into self-contained subsystems that fail to complement one another does not contribute to continuous learning or to a flexible environment that would favor proper skills training in the 21st century.

With the guidance of a mentor, youth in Uruguay should build a middle and higher education career path that flexibly combines foundational content with short specific-training programs, alternating between the two options as required by their individual educational and training needs. Furthermore, the availability of more and better diagnostic and self-assessment tools could guide both the general decisions made on policy (for example, about changing needs in teacher training) and the individual decisions made on training at different stages of youth and adult life.

Teacher training and career development should be reformulated to recruit higher middle education graduates with excellent grades through a policy of stimulus that turns teaching into an appealing option. Teacher training should be a university program that over time requires the completion of postgraduate programs before being licensed for teaching. The teaching career should encompass all pedagogical jobs—such as area directors, pedagogical directors, and developers of teaching materials—and progress in teaching should be based on good performance and permanent training, as well as on seniority.

Teams of highly trained teachers and directors would positively reinforce the autonomy needed by schools allowing them to recruit well-trained teachers by offering incentives to stay for a number of years. School administrators would develop the skills required for making adequate and innovative program and curriculum-related decisions, and directors would be able to choose the staff required to implement them based on the profile of the population for which they work. Pedagogical diagnostic teams would be able to identify students' problems in a timely fashion and implement early intervention programs as required.

A modification to the current system for teacher appointments would increase teachers' connection to their schools, making them members of a stable professional community.[2] Teachers could be required to spend a minimum number of years at one school before moving to another. This requirement could be combined with a system of incentives to reduce the geographical and socioeconomic inequalities of education institutions, with a specially trained team of directors ready to intervene in the most underprivileged environments.

LIFELONG LEARNING TO ADAPT SKILLS TO THE NEW ENVIRONMENT

Technological innovations are affecting the way tasks are done by workers across the economy, as well as creating new tasks and making others obsolete. These trends create changes in labor demand, forcing workers to improve their skills and upgrade their knowledge and abilities to maintain their competitiveness in the market throughout their working lives. This process seems to be incipient in Uruguay, as different factors seem to have softened the impact of innovation on demand for jobs with a high content of routine cognitive tasks, which have increased in recent years.

However, the increase in the content of routine cognitive tasks for jobs in Uruguay presents a challenge in the medium term because these tasks carry automation risk. As automation technologies become standard and their adoption costs decline, the probability of substitution will increase. Because these tasks constitute a large part of the middle-income, average-education worker's job, an employment substitution process could have a negative distributional impact. Hence, policy makers should consider strategies to anticipate these trends, offering retraining to some workers that would go beyond the formal education system and managing task-aging processes to protect the most vulnerable. Uruguay should institute a lifelong learning program that offers training and skills improvement to workers throughout their lives. New skills should correspond to changing labor demand. Implementation does not need to be the exclusive responsibility of the state—although programs should be part of a public policy strategy, the private sector may have an important role in providing on-the-job training and other forms of lifelong learning.

The literature suggests that the results of adult training depend, to a great extent, on prior life experience.[3] Formal education systems are only one of the ways individuals develop their abilities. People spend an average of 30 to 40 years in the labor market, and the investment in human capital over those years is essential to increasing and maintaining productivity. In a constantly transforming labor market, individuals accumulate skills outside the formal education system. The training opportunities that emerge after individuals have entered the labor market are of the utmost importance.

Several factors determine the effectiveness and quality of training during adulthood and working life. Age and education levels play an important role, as younger workers with a higher education level are more likely to learn from their colleagues. The size of the workplace is also relevant; workers in larger companies have more training opportunities.

Continuous training policies should address two realities: (1) the need to assist less-educated workers to close the skills gap that exists between them and those with higher qualifications and (2) the need to offer reskilling to workers in occupations that will likely be subject to task automation. Lifelong learning policies should be addressed to both the employed and the unemployed.

In general, low-quality jobs are closely matched to workers with low human capital. Insufficient human capital affects not only current employment but also an individual's capacity to obtain another job. Employment policies should ensure that people acquire the proper skills to fill positions in a changing and competitive environment. To counteract demographic trends, labor force participation should be increased by incorporating currently inactive persons and upgrading the skills of workers who lost their jobs. Three policy strategies can help achieve this objective. First, intermediation services can provide information and facilitate the link between individuals and potential employers. The second strategy focuses on providing on-the-job training, while the third focuses on more formal training through classes or workshops. Experience in other countries shows that a combination of these approaches maximizes their impact.

Developing an effective skills training program for adult workers is a serious challenge—it requires not only adequate funding but a strategic vision, implementation capacity, and a network of quality providers. The National Institute of Employment and Professional Education (INEFOP), created in 2008, is responsible for public policies aimed at professional training. INEFOP is a tripartite public entity, whose directive council consists of representatives of workers, employers, and the government. Its mandate is to provide professional training activities and monitor productive sectors' demands for qualifications. Although INEFOP is well funded to provide training, its focus is mostly on technical skills that are in high demand in the short term, and not on longer-term strategic reskilling. A growing number of studies note that, in the new labor context, skills in demand go beyond technical or occupation-specific to the realm of softer, basic skills. Employers give priority to workers with basic skills over specifically skilled technical workers. Although these workers may not immediately be ready to work on the required tasks, their flexibility and ability to learn and adapt are more valued (Brown 2002; Guile and Griffiths 2004). These profiles are scarcer in the labor market, and their lack is a barrier to employment for many individuals (Peddle 2000).

These factors have implications for policies promoting the development of active skills. The private sector has incentives to invest in technical skills training for workers with soft and basic skills. Technical skills are not only specific to each productive sector or occupation, but also change over time. Many of these skills are more likely to be developed during an individual's interaction with his or her work environment, and their relationship to a particular job makes it easier for employers to recover their investment in training. On the other hand, soft skills are relevant across the economy, reducing the incentive for individual employers to provide them and requiring a public institution such as INEFOP to take responsibility.

To generate training and education initiatives to help workers and firms adapt to current and future technological changes, the interaction among partic-ipants is crucial; the private sector, unions, education and training institutions, and government must communicate and cooperate to monitor the trends in the demand for skills and provide them effectively when necessary.

ADAPTING LABOR AND SOCIAL PROTECTION REGULATIONS

The emergence of the gig economy poses challenges to policy makers who need to balance strategies to take advantage of the opportunities created by these new technologies with regulations that ensure adequate labor and social protection for workers and their families. The conceptual and empirical discussions presented in this book show that the new forms of employment through crowd-working and on-demand work have the potential advantage of offering a wider and more flexible labor market to individuals who otherwise might be excluded from, or have limited access to, employment opportunities. However, in some cases these new forms of employment are not compatible with existing labor and social protection regulations, which contain restrictions that may reducing labor demand. Labor regulations and social security rules are the state's response, however, to the need to guarantee the basic rights of workers, which would not exist in the absence of these rules.

Most current labor regulations and social security norms in Uruguay were designed around an ideal worker who is a fully registered wage earner, with a long employment history in the same firm, and a family that depends financially on his or her income. Rules concerning severance payments and annual holidays, for example, are linked to the length of employment with the same firm. Pension and health benefits are directly linked to employment history, and other benefits—such as family allowances, unemployment insurance, and even funeral expenses—were traditionally offered only to workers with formal employment. The link between formal employment and access to protection and benefits has softened in recent years, as authorities recognized that the population at risk is not necessarily limited to those employed. Consequently, programs such as family allowances and health insurance have been modified and expanded to include workers and families that are not registered as formal employees, and noncontributory pensions were made more accessible. Although these reforms have not eliminated the link between formal employment and workers' rights, they clearly shifted the policy approach toward a more open model.

This trend might be consistent with the implications of an increasingly gig-based economy: fewer workers in formal, traditional relationships, and more with occasional jobs but still in need of adequate protection. The main debate about labor regulations and social security systems in a changing labor market has focused on whether coverage should be based on employment relationships or whether they should be separated through the establishment of universal noncontributory social protection programs and labor regulations that go beyond traditional employment (Behrendt and Nguyen 2018; World Bank 2019; Packard et al. 2019). Adopting such a model could facilitate employees' entrance and exit from jobs; their rights to social security benefits would no longer be affected, and the higher rotation might result in faster adjustments to changes in the demand for skills by employers. However, these programs could be difficult to finance and have been questioned with respect to their impact on the incentive to work.

Finding a balance between employment-related and noncontributory policies may be a more effective strategy and may be more politically feasible. Most countries have mixed policies, which let them widen the scope of social security and improve the levels of social and economic inclusion of the population. Noncontributory systems are necessary to ensure a basic level of protection for the entire population, especially those with no access to other systems, while contributory systems play a role in the provision of proper benefits, by providing a broader reach and greater protection.

Many digital platform jobs share features with nonstandard forms of employment. Most of them are part-time, temporary jobs, and the line between independent workers and wage earners is not always clear. Some countries have worked, with more or less success, to regulate these labor relations. Given their characteristics, it seems unreasonable to apply the rules and institutional arrangements designed for standard jobs. Instead, those aspects of labor relations that should be regulated or protected should be differentiated from those that, given these specific characteristics, do not require intervention. For example, offering access to pension benefits, labor accident insurance, and rules against discrimination should be mandatory, while implementing other rules usually applied to standard jobs might be more difficult.

Some recommendations are nonspecific for the sector but embrace other more general suggestions for improving working conditions in the most precarious forms of employment. Three significant recommendations are:

- *Adapting social security mechanisms to provide coverage for all forms of employment.* Many of the rules in force were developed for the economies of the industrial era, but they fail to protect workers under nonstandard arrangements (Packard et al. 2019). A policy that sets a minimum set of benefits for all individuals, regardless of their current or former engagement in the labor market, complemented by a contributory program, could effectively offer adequate protection for all. Even where measures have been implemented that extend the systems of contributory social security to workers under nonstandard forms of employment (Spasova et al. 2017; Behrendt and Nguyen 2018), systems based on financing through other noncontributory means can be strengthened to ensure at least some basic coverage for the entire population (Berg et al. 2018; World Bank 2019). Although noncontributory programs have been available in Latin America for decades, the trend in recent years has been unprecedented in its intensity and the speed with which it has spread. Between 2000 and 2013, at least 18 countries in the region introduced inclusive reforms involving noncontributory programs that sought to expand coverage for the elderly. Recent changes appear to be the result of a combination of various factors, including the exhaustion of the contributory model, developed in the second half of the 20th century, for extending statutory coverage; an improvement in the fiscal position of most countries in the region; and social pressure for better-adapted social protection policies with an emphasis on addressing the needs of vulnerable populations (Rofman, Amarante, and Apella 2016).

- *Simplifying and facilitating administrative procedures for registration, making contributions, and paying benefits.* Simplifying and accelerating administrative and financial requirements and procedures may contribute to the coverage of employees (Berg et al. 2018; Behrendt and Nguyen 2018). Simplified tax and contribution systems may be implemented, access to electronic digital platforms may be eased for registration or making queries or payments, and more flexible or fixed contribution systems may be created. Other countries have sought to streamline their social protection systems to facilitate the coverage of self-employed workers, for whom administrative procedures—including registration, income declaration, record-keeping, contribution collection, and benefit payments—are more burdensome. The administrative burden on self-employed workers seeking access to registration could be reduced by opening service centers in rural areas with a high flow of self-employed workers (as in Cabo Verde and Rwanda), reducing the requirement for proof documents (as in Brazil), or introducing autoenrollment (as in Canada, Chile, Italy, and New Zealand) (Berg et al. 2018).

Much of the work on digital platforms is part-time, temporary, and often casual, and the boundaries between genuine self-employment and disguised employment relationships tend to be blurred. Responding to the increasing prevalence of classifying crowdworkers as self-employed, some countries have introduced measures to ensure at least a minimum level of coverage in some areas. For example, France has recently introduced legislation that requires digital platforms to pay occupational accident insurance premiums for self-employed workers who voluntarily or are compelled by the platform to take out such policies, unless the platform has established such insurance through a collective bargaining contract (Huteau and Bonnand 2016).

The registration and payment process can also be simplified by introducing electronic procedures. Uber drivers in Uruguay, for example, can download a smartphone application that automatically deducts social security contributions. Similarly, in Indonesia and Malaysia, taxi drivers, Uber drivers, and Grab drivers can register and make their annual prepayment for employment injury insurance online. In Estonia, Lithuania, and Sweden, Uber drivers can ask Uber to share their fare and other information directly with tax authorities on their behalf, facilitating tax payments for individual drivers and tax collections for tax authorities.

- *Introducing labor regulations and social security rules that consider changes in labor markets.* Most new forms of employment, such as digital platform work and crowdworking, share two basic characteristics: the use of digital technology to assign activities to workers and the flexibility for workers to adjust their work schedule to their needs or wants. Traditional labor regulations make it difficult for these workers to receive adequate protection and benefits. A framework that recognizes innovations—such as a more discontinuous work schedule, partial retirement, or international contracts—would maintain and make more effective several regulatory instruments that, in a black-and-white world, would become inapplicable. Finding an adequate balance between adaptation to new models and security is difficult, but policy makers should face this discussion with an open mind, to search for an equilibrium that will adjust over time.

Proposals for a category of worker between an employee and a freelancer—which different authors call "independent workers" (Harris and Kreuger 2015), "dependent contractors" (Taylor 2017), or "dependent self-employed" workers (Beccaria and Maurizio 2019)—have been discussed. The proposals posit that platform workers should have access to a limited package of benefits and protections. For example, these workers would be entitled to social security coverage but not to the payment of minimum wages. Making these rules clear could reduce potential legal conflicts, although the risk of abusing these regulations to disguise standard salaried jobs as platform work would be high and require strong oversight from authorities (Beccaria and Maurizio 2019).

Crowdworking is global, involving actors across the world. Because both labor regulations and social protection rules are national, the geographical scope of these activities adds a layer of complexity to this discussion. Which regulations should apply? Those from the country where the worker is located, or those where the client is? How can the regulations be supervised and enforced? Different countries have moved toward regulating the worker side of the relationship (including the draft "Service Provision through Information Platforms" law in Uruguay, discussed in Congress in 2016 but not passed), but if international agreements to share information are not available, enforcing these rules will be difficult (Behrendt and Nguyen 2018).

Despite the debate over how to improve employee protection, advantage should be taken of the opportunities that technology offers in new jobs, productivity, efficiency in service supply, and the capacity for service providers to reach a larger number of potential clients at unprecedented scale and speed. Digital platforms allow the connection of multiple individuals and companies almost instantaneously, using only a broadband connection ("scale and no mass"), offering opportunities to millions of individuals anywhere on the globe (Packard et al. 2019).

NOTES

1. Filgueira and Porzecanski (2017) discuss the link between the duration of education cycles and age cycles with respect to the neuronal and biological processes of learning and the acquisition of skills, pointing out the relevance of taking age cycles into account when designing education policies—each stage is essential for the acquisition of certain abilities in a cumulative educational path.
2. Middle education teachers in Uruguay can choose annually where to teach, as well as setting their working schedules with respect to shifts and hours of work, through a seniority-based priority system. This structure leads to an unstable human resources system, weak team building, and regressive effects because the most experienced teachers generally choose schools in the most favorable areas.
3. Berniell et al. (2016).

REFERENCES

Beccaria, L., and R. Maurizio. 2019. "Algunas-reflexiones-en-torno-al-empleo-en-plataformas-y-a-los-mecanismos-de-proteccion." *Alquimias Económicas*, February 27. https://alquimiaseconomicas.com/2019/02/27/algunas-reflexiones-en-torno-al-empleo-en-plataformas-y-a-los-mecanismos-de-proteccion/.

Behrendt, C., and Q. Nguyen. 2018. "Innovative Approaches for Ensuring Universal Social Protection for Future of Work." ILO Future of Work Research Paper Series, International

Labour Organization, Geneva. https://www.ilo.org/wcmsp5/groups/public/---dgreports/---cabinet/documents/publication/wcms_629864.pdf.

Berg, J., M. Furrer, E. Harmon, U. Rani, and M. S. Silberman. 2018. *Digital Labour Platforms and the Future of Work: Towards Decent Work in the Online World*. Geneva: International Labour Organization. https://www.ilo.org/wcmsp5/groups/public/---dgreports/---dcomm/---publ/documents/publication/wcms_645337.pdf.

Berniell, L., D. de la Mata, R. Bernal, A. Camacho, F. Barrera-Osorio, F. Álvarez, P. Brassiolo, and J. Vargas. 2016. *RED 2016: Más habilidades para el trabajo y la vida— los aportes de la familia, la escuela, el entorno y el mundo laboral.* Bogotá: CAF. http://scioteca.caf.com/handle/123456789/936.

Brown, B. L. 2002. *CTE Student Organizations. ERIC Digest 235.* Columbus, OH: ERIC Clearinghouse on Adult, Career, and Vocational Education.

Dutz, M., R. Almeida, and T. Packard. 2018. *The Jobs of Tomorrow: Technology, Productivity, and Prosperity in Latin America and the Caribbean.* Directions in Development. Washington, DC: World Bank. https://openknowledge.worldbank.org/handle/10986/29617.

Filgueira, F., and A. Porzecanski. 2017. "Aging, the Knowledge Economy and Human Capital Creation in Latin America from Early Childhood to Secondary Education: Old and New Challenges." Background paper, World Bank, Washington, DC.

Guile, D., and T. Griffiths. 2001. "Learning through Work Experience." *Journal of Education and Work* 14 (1): 113–31.

Harris, S., and B. Kreuger. 2015. "A Proposal for Modernizing Labor Laws for Twenty-First-Century Work: The 'Independent Worker.'" Discussion Paper 2015-10, Brookings Institution, Washington, DC.

Huteau, G., and G. Bonnand. 2016. "France." In *ESPN Thematic Report on Access to Social Protection of People Working as Self-Employed or on Non-Standard Contracts.* Brussels: European Commission.

Kärkkäinen, K. 2012. "Bringing About Curriculum Innovations: Implicit Approaches in the OECD Area." OECD Education Working Paper 82, Organisation for Economic Co-operation and Development, Paris. https://doi.org/10.1787/5k95qw8xzl8s-en.

Packard, T., U. Gentilini, M. Grosh, P. O'Keefe, R. Palacios, D. Robalino and I. Santos. 2019. *Protecting All: Risk Sharing for a Diverse and Diversifying World of Work.* Washington, DC: World Bank. doi: 10.1596/978-1-4648-1427-3.

Peddle, M. T. 2000. "Frustration at the Factory: Employer Perceptions of Workforce Deficiencies and Training Trends." *Journal of Regional Analysis and Policy* 30 (1): 23–40. http://www.jrap-journal.org/pastvolumes/2000/v30/30-1-2.pdf.

Rofman, R., V. Amarante, and I. Apella. 2016. *Demographic Change in Uruguay: Economic Opportunities and Challenges.* Directions in Development. Washington, DC: World Bank. https://openknowledge.worldbank.org/handle/10986/24358.

Spasova, S., D. Bouget, D. Ghailani, and V. Vanhercke. 2017. *Access to Social Protection for People Working on Non-Standard Contracts and as Self-Employed in Europe: A Study of National Policies.* Brussels: European Commission. https://ec.europa.eu/social/main.jsp?langId=en&catId=1135&newsId=2798&furtherNews=yes.

Taylor, M. 2017. *Good Work: The Taylor Review of Modern Working Practices.* London: Department for Business, Energy & Industrial Strategy.

World Bank. 2018. *World Development Report 2018: Learning to Realize Education's Promise.* Washington, DC: World Bank. https://openknowledge.worldbank.org/handle/10986/28340.

World Bank. 2019. *World Development Report 2019: The Changing Nature of Work.* Washington, DC: World Bank. https://openknowledge.worldbank.org/handle/10986/30435.

Conclusion

Population aging and technological change are shaping labor markets around the world. Although both trends have positive implications, they also present risks that should be addressed by public policy. The demographic trends result from lower mortality and fertility, which follow from sustained improvements in welfare and offer demographic dividends. However, in the medium term these trends will result in significant increases in dependency ratios, which must be offset by growing productivity. Technological change could be a force for the long-term increase in productivity but may put at risk employment for many workers and promote labor polarization.

This book shows that both trends are relevant and already under way in Uruguay. The population is aging and opportunities to take advantage of the demographic dividend must be seized now, increasing labor force participation and national savings. Technological innovations are also gradually advancing in different sectors of the economy. Although this process is not homogeneous (across the economy, some sectors are moving faster than others, and there are variations within sectors and value chains), the effects on labor demand are visible and could grow in the medium term.

Recognizing risks and opportunities is the first step in managing them. New technology creates industries and areas of employment that did not exist even a few years ago. It also reduces employment in some occupations by replacing human work with automation in specific tasks, but evidence shows that these reductions may be offset by a scale effect triggered by a reduction in costs produced by the innovations. This process is rarely considered when governments design and implement sectoral promotion policies, which are usually targeted to sectors that may increase exports, reduce imports, or contribute to total growth; its inclusion in policy design should have a positive impact.

Even if, thanks to scale effects, labor demand grows with innovations, providing current and future workers with the necessary skills to compete for these new jobs is critical. An effective education system should provide access to education for all, ensure that learning processes are effective in the classroom, and ensure that the subjects taught are relevant for students' futures. The current education system in Uruguay has serious issues in all three factors, with high dropout rates in basic education that result from cumulative skill deficits, quality issues, and critical issues with the relevance of the curriculum.

A combination of deep reform in the governance of the sector, improvements in the quality of preservice and in-service training for teachers, and a revision of curricula to reflect the demand for current skills are critical to building an education system that produces a competitive labor force for this century. Uruguay has a well-funded institution for retraining and reskilling those already in the labor force; its focus should be on providing necessary skills to current middle-age workers.

Finally, labor market regulations and social insurance rules should be adapted to evolving labor markets. These norms and institutions were designed for an archetypal worker who is slowly disappearing. Formally employed workers who stay in the same firm for years, have family depending on their income, and retire in their sixties after a 35–40 year working career were never the norm in Uruguay, and now some of the rules are gradually becoming even less relevant. Providing adequate protection to workers is a core obligation for the government, but making the rules more flexible to include an increasingly heterogeneous labor force is critical for the medium term.

Although technological change is a phenomenon that has been happening at an accelerating pace in the last two decades, the penetration of technology that replaces routine cognitive tasks currently performed by mid-skilled and medium-wage workers has not been significant. Uruguay is in a good position to anticipate shocks and develop sectoral promotion policies, adapt its education and lifelong learning systems, and update labor regulation and social insurance programs to take advantage of opportunities and moderate the negative effects these changes may bring.

Additional Reading

Almeida, R., L. Anazawa, N. M. Filho, and L. Vasconcellos. 2015. "Investing in Technical and Vocational Education and Training: Does It Yield Large Economic Returns in Brazil?" Policy Research Working Paper 7246. Washington, DC: World Bank Group. https://openknowledge .worldbank.org/handle/10986/21861.

Andreasson, K. 2009. *Global Education 20/20: What Role for the Private Sector?* London: Economist Intelligence Unit. http://graphics.eiu.com/marketing/pdf/Cisco_Education _2020.pdf.

Bentaouet Kattan, R., K. Macdonald, and H. A. Patrinos. 2018. "Automation and Labor Market Outcomes: The Pivotal Role of High-Quality Education." Policy Research Working Paper 8474. Washington, DC: World Bank Group. https://openknowledge.worldbank.org /handle/10986/29903.

Blinder, A. S, 1973. "Wage Discrimination: Reduced Form and Structural Estimates." *Journal of Human Resources* 8 (4): 436–55.

Booth, R., 2016. *The Guardian* [online]. https://www.theguardian.com/technology/2016 /dec/14/uber-appeals-against-ruling-that-its-uk-drivers-are-employees.

Brynjolfsson, E., and A. McAfee. 2012. *Race against the Machine: How the Digital Revolution Is Accelerating Innovation, Driving Productivity, and Irreversibly Transforming Employment and the Economy.* Cambridge, MA: MIT Center for Digital Business.

Brynjolfsson, E., and A. McAfee. 2014. *The Second Machine Age: Work, Progress, and Prosperity in a Time of Brilliant Technologies.* London and New York: W.W. Norton & Company.

Carneiro, P., and J. J. Heckman., 2003. "Human Capital Policy." IZA Discussion Paper 821. Institute for the Study of Labor (IZA). http://ftp.iza.org/dp821.pdf.

Casner-Lotto, J., and L. Barrington. 2006. *Are They Really Ready to Work? Employers' Perspectives on the Basic Knowledge and Applied Skills of New Entrants to the 21st Century US Workforce.* Washington DC: Partnership for 21st Century Skills. https://files .eric.ed.gov/fulltext/ED519465.pdf.

Cunningham, W., M. Parra Torrado, and M. Sarzosa. 2016. "Cognitive and Non-Cognitive Skills for the Peruvian Labor Market: Addressing Measurement Error through Latent Skills Estimations." Policy Research Working Paper 7550. Washington, DC: World Bank Group. https://openknowledge.worldbank.org/bitstream/handle/10986/23725 /Cognitive0and00t0skills0estimations.pdf?sequence=1&isAllowed=y.

Dos Santos, C. 2018. El Observador [online]. https://www.elobservador.com.uy/nota/crean -sindicato-de-deliveries-se-juntaban-en-una-plaza-en-rivera-y-soca-y-ya-son -170-repartidores-2018810500.

Goldin, C., and L. Katz. 2009. *The Race Between Education and Technology.* Cambridge, MA: Harvard University Press.

INE (Instituto Nacional de Estadística). 2013. *Encuesta Nacional de Adolescencia y Juventud.* http://www.ine.gub.uy/encuesta-nacional-de-adolescencia-y-juventud.

INE (Instituto Nacional de Estadística). 2019. *Encuesta Continua de Hogares.* http://www.ine .gub.uy/encuesta-continua-de-hogares.

Mourshed, M., D. Farrell, and D. Barton. 2012. *Education to Employment: Designing a System That Works.* McKinsey Center for Government. Washington, DC: McKinsey & Company. https://www.mckinsey.com/~/media/McKinsey/Industries/Social%20Sector/Our%20 Insights/Education%20to%20employment%20Designing%20a%20system%20that%20 works/Education%20to%20employment%20designing%20a%20system%20that%20 works.ashx.

Mueller, G., and E. J. S. Plug, 2006. "Estimating the Effect of Personality on Male and Female Earnings." *Industrial and Labor Relations Review* 60 (1): 3–22. http://digitalcommons.ilr .cornell.edu/ilrreview/vol60/iss1/1.

Oaxaca, R, 1973. "Male-Female Wage Differentials in Urban Labor Markets." *International Economic Review* 14 (3): 693–709. https://web.sonoma.edu/users/c/cuellar/econ421 /oaxaca.pdf.

OECD (Organisation for Economic Co-operation and Development). 2004. *The PISA 2003 Assessment Framework: Mathematics, Reading, Science and Problem-Solving Knowledge and Skills,* http://www.oecd.org/edu/preschoolandschool/programmefor internationalstudentassessmentpisa/33694881.pdf.

OECD (Organisation for Economic Co-operation and Development). 2017. *Getting Skills Right: Skills for Jobs Indicators.* Paris: OECD Publishing. http://dx.doi.org/10.1787/9789264277878 -en.

Vee, A. 2017. "Coding Literacy: How Computer Programming Is Changing Writing." *Software Studies.* Cambridge, MA: MIT Press.

Zeballos, A., and E. Iglesias Rodríguez. 2017. *Digital Economy in Latin America and the Caribbean: Current Situation and Recommendations.* New York: Inter-American Development Bank.

Technological Change: Banco de la República Oriental del Uruguay

TABLE A.1 **Technological change: Banco de la República Oriental del Uruguay**

	DIGITAL CHANNEL			CORRESPONDENT FINANCIAL INSTITUTIONS[a]
eBROU	AppBROU	TELEPHONE BANKING	RedBROU (ATMs)	
Reasons for implementing the channel				
Cost reduction	n.a.	n.a.	Cost reduction	Cost reduction
n.a.		n.a.	n.a.	Staff reduction
n.a.	Labor factor productivity increase	Labor factor productivity increase	Labor factor productivity increase	n.a.
Competitive advantage over competitors	n.a.	Competitive advantage over competitors	Competitive advantage over competitors	n.a.
Vision of future market	n.a.	n.a.	n.a.	n.a.
n.a.	Security and transparency improvement	n.a.	Security and transparency improvement	n.a.
n.a.	n.a.	n.a.	n.a.	Benefiting from fully or partially unsatisfied demand
n.a.	n.a.	n.a.	n.a.	Regulatory changes
n.a.	n.a.	Image improvement	24-hour availability	n.a.
Investments made to develop the channel				
n.a.	n.a.	Machinery and equipment acquisition	Machinery and equipment acquisition	n.a.
n.a.	n.a.	Hardware acquisition	Hardware acquisition	n.a.
Software acquisition	Software acquisition	Software acquisition	Software acquisition	n.a.
License or patent acquisition	License or patent acquisition	License or patent acquisition	License or patent acquisition	n.a.
Consultant hiring	Consultant hiring	Consultant hiring	n.a.	n.a.
n.a.	n.a.	n.a.	Transaction entities	New figures with existing technologies
Consequences of channel implementation				
Cost reduction	n.a.	Cost reduction	Cost reduction	Cost reduction
Staff reduction	n.a.	n.a.	Staff reduction	Staff reduction

continued

TABLE A.1, *continued*

DIGITAL CHANNEL				
eBROU	**AppBROU**	**TELEPHONE BANKING**	**RedBROU (ATMs)**	**CORRESPONDENT FINANCIAL INSTITUTIONS**[a]
Competitive advantage over competitors	Competitive advantage over competitors	Competitive advantage over competitors	Competitive advantage over competitors	Competitive advantage over competitors
Labor factor productivity increase	n.a.	n.a.	Labor factor productivity increase	Labor factor productivity increase
Security and transparency improvement	Security and transparency improvement	Security and transparency improvement	Security and transparency improvement	n.a.
Stage of organizational change				
Reengineering	n.a.	n.a.	n.a.	n.a.
n.a.	Automation	n.a.	Automation	Automation
n.a.	n.a.	Rationalization	Rationalization	Rationalization
Available workforce				
n.a.	Had the necessary professional training and skills	Had the necessary professional training and skills	n.a.	Had the necessary professional training and skills

Source: Aboal et al. 2019.
Note: eBROU and AppBROU are e-banking services of Banco de la República Oriental del Uruguay (BROU). RedBROU is BROU's system of automated teller machines (ATMs); n.a. = not applicable.
a. Payment and collection networks through third parties, such as Abitab and Redpagos.

Decomposition Based on Recentered Influence Functions (RIF) Regressions

The decomposition method proposed by Firpo, Fortin, and Lemieux (2011) is based on a regression estimate where labor income—the independent variable— is replaced with a transformation thereon, the recentered influence function (RIF). The RIF enables the measurement, in distributional statistics such as deciles, of the effect of small changes in the underlying distribution. A great advantage of this type of decomposition is that it enables the calculation of the unconditional marginal effect of marginal changes in an explanatory variable of labor income from different parts of the distribution.

Following Firpo, Fortin, and Lemieux (2011), for each decile of the labor income distribution FY, $v(F)$ measures the importance of each observation in the conformation of the value of such statistic. In general terms, an RIF-regression coefficient can be interpreted as the contribution of one observation to the individual statistic of interest:

$$RIF(Y) = v(F) + IF(Y) \qquad (1)$$

In the case of quantiles, the influence function $IF(Y; Q_\tau)$ is given by $(\tau - I\{Y \le Q_\tau\})/f_Y(Q_\tau)$, where $I\{\cdot\}$ is an indicator function, $f_Y(\cdot)$ is the density of the marginal distribution of Y, and Q_τ is the population quantile of the unconditional distribution of Y. Therefore, $RIF(Y; Q_\tau)$ equals $Q_\tau + IF(Y; Q_\tau)$, and can be rewritten as:

$$RIF(Y;Q_\tau) = Q_\tau + \frac{\tau - I\{Y \le Q_\tau\}}{f_Y(Q_\tau)} = c_{1,\tau} \cdot I\{Y > Q_\tau\} + c_{2,\tau}, \qquad (2)$$

Where $c_{1,\tau} = 1/f_Y(Q_\tau)$, and $c_{2,\tau} = Q_\tau - c_{1,\tau}(1 - \tau)$. We can observe, then, that except for the constants $c_{1,\tau}$ and $c_{2,\tau}$, the RIF for a quantile is simply an indicator $I\{Y \le Q_\tau\}$ when the outcome variable is smaller than or equal to the quantile of interest. In other words, the RIF can be computed empirically through a local inversion that specifies whether the value Y is smaller than or equal to Q_τ. After calculating the RIF for the statistic of interest, we obtain a value of the variable transformed for each observation of the sample. These values are used to estimate a regression of ordinary least squares (OLS) of the RIF variable in a vector of explanatory variables under the assumption that the conditioned expected value of the RIF function can be shaped as a linear function of the explanatory variables, and that the effect of the change in the distribution of an explanatory variable in the statistic can be expressed, ceteris paribus, as the average partial effect of that variable on the conditioned expected value of its RIF function. The coefficients obtained in the OLS regression can, therefore, be interpreted as the effect of an increase in the mean of an explanatory variable in the quantile of interest.

Specifically, this study estimates two sets of unconditional regressions where the explanatory variables include workers' observable characteristics, such as age, educational level, and economic activity sector; and five variables that have (approximately) a zero mean and variance equal to 1, according to the task-content of each ISCO-08 occupation and that capture the occupational intensity in tasks classified as routine cognitive, routine manual, nonroutine cognitive–analytical, nonroutine cognitive–interpersonal, and nonroutine manual.

The estimated coefficients in the regression described above are used to calculate a standard Oaxaca-Blinder decomposition in each statistic. This decomposition can be described as follows:

$$\Delta_v = \left(\overline{X}_s - \overline{X}_t\right)\hat{\theta}_v^* + \left\{\overline{X}_s\left(\hat{\theta}_{t,v} - \hat{\theta}_v^*\right) + \overline{X}_t\left(\hat{\theta}_v^* - \hat{\theta}_{s,v}\right)\right\} \tag{3}$$

Where Δ_v represents the difference in the statistic v between the wage distributions for the years t and s; $\overline{X}_t$ and $\overline{X}_s$ are the average characteristics of each year; and $\hat{\theta}_{s,v}$ and $\hat{\theta}_{t,v}$ denote the coefficients estimated on the basis of the RIF regression of the statistic v over the set of explanatory variables for the years t and s. The first component of the equation, $\left(\overline{X}_s - \overline{X}_t\right)\hat{\theta}_v^*$, is the effect of the differences in the statistic of the difference in characteristics, also known as the "explained" component or composition effect. The second component, $\overline{X}_s(\hat{\theta}_{t,v} - \hat{\theta}_v^*) + \overline{X}_t(\hat{\theta}_v^* - \hat{\theta}_{s,v})$, known as the "unexplained" component, belongs to the effect of changes in coefficients.

REFERENCES

Aboal, D., A. López, R. Maurizio, P. Queraltó, and E. Tealde. 2019. "Digitalización y empleo en Uruguay en los sectores bancario, forestal y supermercados: Impactos y estrategias para la adaptación del capital humano." Background paper, World Bank, Washington, DC.

Firpo, S., N. M. Fortin, and T. Lemieux. 2011. "Occupational Tasks and Changes in the Wage Structure." IZA Discussion Paper 5542, Institute for the Study of Labor, Bonn. http://ftp.iza.org/dp5542.pdf.